Listening Hearts

Listening Hearts

Fourteen Gatherings for Reflection and Sharing

Christine Robinson and Alicia Hawkins

SKINNER HOUSE BOOKS
BOSTON

Published by Skinner House Books, an imprint of the Unitarian Universalist Association, a liberal religious organization with more than 1,000 congregations in the U.S. and Canada, 24 Farnsworth St., Boston, MA 02210–1409.

www.skinnerhouse.org

Printed in the United States

Cover and text design by Suzanne Morgan
Cover art *Circuition 13*, © Tracey Adams, www.traceyadamsart.com

print ISBN: 978-1-55896-768-7
eBook ISBN: 978-1-55896-769-4

6 5 4 3 2 1
18 17 16 15

Library of Congress Cataloging-in-Publication Data

Robinson, Christine C.
Listening hearts : fourteen gatherings for reflection and sharing / Christine Robinson and Alicia Hawkins.
     pages cm
  Includes bibliographical references.
    ISBN 978-1-55896-768-7 (pbk. : alk. paper) — ISBN 978-1-55896-769-4 (ebook) 1. Spiritual life—Unitarian Universalist Association. 2. Church group work—Unitarian Universalist Association. I. Title.
  BX9855.R625 2015
  253'.7—dc23
                              2015026233

Credit lines for copyrighted material listed on page 160.

Contents

Acknowledgments

This book was written with the help and support of many people, foremost our husbands, William Baker and Charlie Hawkins. Many participants in the covenant groups at First Unitarian Church in Albuquerque helped to field test these gatherings. In addition, we are grateful for our partnership in the writing of this book. Christine Robinson wrote the essays and Alicia Hawkins supplied quotes, poems, and readings and kept on top of the logistics of our project.

Foreword

I felt as lifeless as one of those Middle Eastern deserts you see in *National Geographic*, just hill after hill of hot sand, without a tree or a bit of vegetation to break up the view. My baby daughter had just completed six months of chemotherapy for kidney cancer. She was returning to health; my spirit was not. I had lost all faith and sense of meaning. As far as I was concerned, not only was there no God, there was no purpose. I had no answers to any of the important questions of life.

Feeling so deeply alone, I began attending a covenant group at my home church. The gentle atmosphere, the support of the other members as they listened without correcting or debating, and their willingness to be vulnerable and share their stories allowed me to find my own answers—ones that fit my "new normal."

Slowly but surely, my parched spirit healed. The shallow, facile theology that had made up my previous worldview began to fade away. Held in this compassionate group, I was able, one by one, to put together the beliefs that I found to be true and life-giving. In that covenanted group, I could test new ideas by voicing them aloud, while being afforded the privilege of hearing the other group members voice their own tender beliefs.

When rough times came again, as they inevitably do, I had developed by then a solid foundation to help me weather the storm. I owned a tested system of belief and an internal strength that was fed by a group, committed to creating sacred space in our time together.

Some say that covenant groups (also called chalice circles or small group ministries) are a conversion experience. Both through my personal experience and my experience as a minister witnessing others in their first covenant group, I have found this to be true. In addition to my story, I can tell you about countless others and how covenant groups have transformed their lives. But when you experience it firsthand, it makes you want to shout from the mountaintops about the power of the small group.

A covenant group is like a gym for the soul. As a participant, you get to exercise "what it means to be human," to use a phrase from Unitarian luminary James Luther Adams. Your mini-community models mutual respect, as members practice deeply listening to one another. Your spirit becomes stronger as you stretch to accommodate new ideas, as you wrestle with your own conclusions, and as you learn how to compassionately hold the space for another member to process their own experiences.

Join or form a covenant group. Your life will be better. *You* will be better. *Listening Hearts* provides everything leaders and participants need to run these kinds of spiritual and emotional sharing groups. Resting on a foundation of two previous books, *Heart to Heart* and *Soul to Soul*, it makes leadership easy and helps groups engage in the kinds of meaningful conversations in which people find meaning and transform, and even save, their lives.

—Joanna Fontaine Crawford

Minister, Live Oak Unitarian Universalist Congregation in Austin, Texas, and the mother of four (all now healthy!) children

Introduction

This is the third in a series of books of resources for spiritual sharing groups, sometimes called covenant groups or chalice circles. These gatherings may form within congregations or in other settings, such as groups of friends or family. The book uses the same format as its predecessors, *Heart to Heart* and *Soul to Soul*, with quotations, an essay, and questions to ponder on fourteen different topics, as well as an easy-to-lead session plan that helps groups form quickly and experience deep sharing and deep listening.

People who enjoy participating in these kinds of small groups do so because it helps them to quench a thirst, find meaning, and have an authentic experience. Many participants say that in the small group setting they feel truly heard for the first time. They share with others in a dialogue about meaningful topics and they feel safe to be completely themselves.

How the Program Works

Groups often form in congregations with the goal of exploring spiritual or life issues and deepening relationships. You can also assemble a group of friends, or even use this book at a family gathering. Six to eight people is an ideal size for a group. But you can also use this book by yourself, with journal in hand.

We recommend that you explore the topics in the order that they appear, as some concepts recur. Meeting for ninety minutes at a time, twice a month, works very well. Weekly meetings, though often impractical, are even better. Other models include meeting on a monthly basis or covering several topics during a weekend retreat. Each participant will need a copy of this book.

Each gathering explores a different topic with an essay, quotations, and questions. Participants should read the chapter and do the preparatory work before the gathering. The quotations invite you to view the topic through various perspectives and serve as a brief introduction to the topic. The Consider This essay fleshes out the topic and gives some structure to exploring it as a group. Finally, the Activities & Questions section helps participants internalize the topic; some people write their responses to the questions in a journal, some scribble comments in the book margins, and some read and ponder the questions over the days or weeks before the gathering. Early preparation by participants will enable the topic to "brew." We encourage you to reflect on as many questions as you feel comfortable with, especially those that speak to you. Thinking about the topic beforehand allows participants to go deeper into the subject matter when sharing about it in the group context.

Leadership

The format of the gatherings was developed to make it easy to be the group leader. The leader does the work of assembling the group and introducing the participants to the format. Most sessions follow the same format and rules, making it easy for the group to become comfortable with the flow of the gathering.

At the back of this book, beginning on page 141, you'll find a Leader's Guide, with general advice for leaders and instructions for certain segments of the gatherings (the opening and closing rituals, ways of experiencing the time of silence, etc.), plus ways to deal with tricky issues. Leaders should read this before the first gathering. Some of the gatherings require special instructions for leaders. These can be found in Leader's Notes for Particular Gatherings on page 153 and should be checked by the leader before each gathering.

Once the group has solidified, many groups share the role of leader. This is a positive development in most groups. The original leader should always be alert to oversee the program and deal with any problems that arise.

The Gatherings

Each gathering has a consistent structure in order to promote a feeling of safety and to encourage interpersonal bonding. Deep listening and sharing make up the core of the gathering and this will be explained in detail at the first meeting. Each gathering has the following components:

Words of the Day

Opening Ritual (which includes chalice lighting, sharing the words of the day, and a responsive reading)

On Our Hearts (a brief sharing of general highs and lows in members' lives)

Silence

Shared Readings

Sharing (two rounds of sharing by members on the specific topic)

Closing Ritual (which includes participants sharing a few words about how they are feeling or an insight gained, extinguishing the chalice, and ending with a moment of silence, a song, or a gong from a bowl or chime)

Announcements

Before the First Gathering

The leader will inform participants about the meeting time and place. Prior to arriving, participants should do the following:

- Obtain a copy of this book and read the Foreword and the Introduction. If this is not possible, you will be able to purchase a copy of the book at the meeting.

- Think about why you were drawn to this group. Be prepared to share your response with the group.
- Bring three photos of yourself. These might include a picture from your infancy or childhood years, one of you as a teenager or young adult, and one current picture. Or bring any three photos that will help you introduce yourself to the group. You will only have about five minutes to share, so be selective.

As you begin this journey in community, listening, growth, and trust, we wish you well. We hope you will find spiritual enrichment and form deep friendships through this experience.

THANK YOU FOR YOUR LOVING HANDS

Music: Judy Fjell ©1982 Lyrics: Lisa Bregger & Judy Fjell©2000

ONE

Snapshots of Our Lives

∽

GATHERING

Words of the Day

I was drawn to this group because . . .

Chalice Lighting

We light this chalice (candle, lamp, etc.) to shine on our time together. In its light we celebrate the relationships and understanding we are creating in this place and time. May our sharing be deep. [Light chalice.]

The Basket

Responsive Reading

Leader: The words we share . . .

Response: *come from our hearts, our minds, our lives.*

Leader: The feelings we express . . .

Response: *are real, important, and a part of the human heritage we all share.*

Leader: The ties we create in this community . . .

Response: *remind us of the web of creation, of which we are a part.*

Silence   3 minutes

Business   10 minutes

Covenant and Ground Rules

I commit myself:
- to come to meetings when I possibly can, knowing that my presence is important to the group
- to let the leader know if I will be absent or need to quit
- to share with the leader the responsibility for good group process by watching how much time I take to speak and noticing what is going on for others
- to do the reading and think about the topic ahead of time
- to not gossip about what is shared in the group and tell only my own story to others
- to honor the safety of the group by listening to what others share with an open heart
- to refrain from cross-talk, judging, or giving advice
- to share as deeply as I can when it is my turn

Introducing the Sharing   10 minutes

There are two rounds of sharing. During each round, one person speaks at a time. The job of listeners is to listen deeply, keeping their hearts open. The speakers share from the heart as deeply as they are willing.

Round 1: Each person in the group takes five to six minutes to reflect aloud on the quotations, essay, and the subject, sharing their own personal experiences about the topic. The leader starts. Everyone who wants to speak gets one turn, in whatever order they choose. Anyone may pass. At the conclusion of a participant's comments, the group leader may say thank you, but there is no further discussion, just a few breaths of silence. Then the next person speaks.

Round 2: This is an opportunity to share "second thoughts" as well as thoughts prompted by what others have shared. The speaker still focuses on their own thoughts, feelings, and experiences—this is not about debating issues. Everyone who wants to speak gets a turn, in whatever order they choose, until the time runs out. It's everybody's responsibility to ensure that all who want to speak get a chance and that no one is dominating.

Sharing   60 minutes

Closing Circle

Extinguishing the Chalice

We extinguish this flame, and we remember the warmth of our community, the light of our wisdom, the generosity of our sharing. We keep these in our heart until we meet again. [Extinguish the chalice.]

Song/Silence

Announcements

TWO

Sanctuary

❧

BEFORE YOU GATHER

A sanctuary is a place of refuge from danger, threat, injury, and fear. It has been recognized since ancient times—and scientific research has validated—that for physical and emotional healing to occur, people need such a protected space in order to allow time, healers, and the natural powers of recovery to work their magic.
—Sandra L. Bloom and Brian Farragher

Indeed, sometimes we are so worn out by our daily activities that we forget to notice our need for recharging. Renewal is a profound tonic. With sanctuary and rest, we can prepare to go forth again.
—Deng Ming-Dao

All of humanity needs ways of dealing with our fears and anxieties. We all need to be in a relationship. We need to feel safe. We need a caring group to which we can belong. Everyone needs comfort, kindness, love, support, and reassurance. . . . We need places where, and people with whom we can address questions about life.
—Walter Kania

The ache for home lives in all of us, the safe place where we can go as we are and not be questioned.

—Maya Angelou

Consider This

A minister once posted a sign on the doors of her ornate New England church that said, simply, "Sanctuary: n. -a refuge for wildlife." Her congregation was a little taken aback. They took their lovely worship space for granted and had never equated it with safety or thought of themselves as needing protection. The sign grew on them, however, and helped them to value their building and what happened in it in a new way.

Our lives are chancy, with changes and challenges always awaiting us. The more stresses and dangers we face in our lives, the more we need to cultivate relative places of safety and rest, places where we can relax without immediate danger, where our voices are heard, where our personhood is respected, where we can let down our guard and be as free as possible from anxieties about life's misfortunes.

We vulnerable human beings need to feel safe to be healthy. While our bodies equip us, via hormones and other brain chemicals, to face or flee danger with remarkable strength when necessary, we are not so well equipped to be on this kind of alert hour after hour or day after day. When we feel constantly pressured by small dangers that we can't do much about, such as traffic or abusive co-workers, the same danger chemicals flood our bodies and do us real harm. We need regular doses of safety to encourage our bodies to stand down, relax, and repair.

We also need to feel that sense of safety to pursue many of the good things of our lives—recreation, caring for others, spiritual fulfillment, creativity, and learning. Hence our need for sanctuaries and refuges, loving families, and safe relationships. We lock our doors, make agreements with those we live and work with, establish rules in our groups, and, if we are wise, practice finding a safe, calm space in our own minds and hearts.

There are several kinds of sanctuaries: places, structures (such as just laws), relationships, and our inner world. We need them all.

The original meaning of the word *sanctuary* is a container for the Holy, or a place where God is. But over the centuries the word has also come to mean a safe place, a place of refuge. Whether or not you resonate with the idea that the Holy is more present in some places than others, this newer definition of the word is theologically neutral, while it also suggests the critical importance of safe places in our lives.

Our safe places certainly can include spaces for public worship (another common use of the word *sanctuary*). Indeed, unless a worship room begins to feel safe to those who use it, it will not serve its purpose well, for it will be difficult to relax into the mood of open receptivity that is the hallmark of worship. This is one reason that visitors to a new congregation, or congregations in a new worship space, or even congregations facing a change in their worship routine, often don't like what they experience at first. Until we know what to expect and can quit scanning our environment for the unexpected, we will have a hard time moving inward, learning, or even focusing. Our experience of worship will feel disjointed, shallow, and unsatisfactory. Familiarity and comfort solve this problem over time, and when we can relax and experience the precious sense of worship, a sanctuary becomes not only a safe place but a container for the Holy.

We often experience other places in our lives as sanctuaries. Many of us want our homes to be a sanctuary from the stresses and dangers of the outside world. This is not only a matter of locking the door behind us but of putting thought and resources into making our home the kind of place where we can relax and be fully ourselves. This often involves matching our space with ourselves, with an eye to our needs and comforts, tastes and individuality. To feel safe, we need to feel known, accounted for, and valued. The child's room that is painted her favorite color, the basement that is carefully set up for the teenager's gaming group, the corner for crafts in the living room, or the flowers always displayed on the apartment's entryway—these kinds of small touches make a home a sanctuary for those who live there together.

Public spaces can be sanctuary-like. Libraries are often meant to be so; librarians want patrons to be able to focus on their reading or study without having to worry about threats. Gardens and parks can feel like sanctuaries to nature-lovers. In most cases, architects or designers hope that these public spaces feel safe and sanctuary-like, but it's a process, not a guarantee. Places can be designed to be sanctuaries, but they only become them as they grow on us, evolving into places where we feel free to take refuge from the world. This happens not through any particular proclamation but through the way places are used and how we come to feel when we enter them. It's a creative process between the space and the people who use it. A sanctuary can be spoiled for an individual or a group if too many discomforting things happen there, and then, even after safety is restored, it must become sanctuary-like again in the minds and hearts of those who use it—either by ritual or with the healing power of time. If the sanctuary of our home has been violated, perhaps by a robbery, we are eager to restore not only its broken doors or windows but our feeling of safety within it. We clean up, we bring in flowers, we ask friends to come and fill the space with laughter, conversation, and the vibrations of peace, or perhaps have a ritual such as smudging, candle lighting, or blessing.

Part of what makes spaces feel safe is our trust in the people who are in them with us. To that end, customs and agreements let us know what we can expect from those around us and assess how safe we are. A work or personal sharing group may make agreements about who may speak and what is shared and what may be said outside the group. Families often have similar "family rules" that keep family communication healthy. A betrayal of these rules and agreements is a betrayal of trust that affects not only the one who was betrayed but the whole group. Once the problems have been hashed out and new agreements made, sometimes the group invents a ritual or ceremony to restore trust. After a tough family meeting, dessert is brought out, perhaps, or tea served or hands held, a prayer said, or a round of hugs given and received. These rituals augment what our rational minds have experienced with the kinds of activities that speak to our hearts.

When new families or groups gather and begin their life together, they may make explicit or implicit agreements about how they are going to be together, hopefully in ways that maximize everyone's sense of safety. However, most people don't start feeling safe with a new group right away or just because of agreements made. They act tentatively until they have experienced how the group really manages itself. It's only after the successful negotiation of a few dangers or problems together that a group can relax and really feel safe. Often, that is when the deepest relationships tend to begin.

Another layer of meaning in this laden word, *sanctuary*, comes from a legal practice beginning in medieval Europe, in which suspected criminals could take refuge in a church and remain safe from arrest and punishment. In the days when laws were often enforced by mobs or informal leaders with little accountability, there was wide trust of the church. The practice of sanctuary gave a chance for tempers to cool and justice to prevail. Later in Europe, when the winning of a battle by one side left many warriors in enemy territory, defeated warriors took shelter in churches so that they would be safe until transport to their own lands could be negotiated. This is how the word that originally meant "a container for the Holy" came to imply "a safe place."

Today we sometimes refer to political sanctuaries, when a person who is endangered for their political views in one nation is offered refuge in another nation. Here in the United States, there have been two sanctuary movements; one in the 1980s, when religious groups sheltered undocumented refugees from Central America who had fled political chaos there, and another in the 2010s, when religious groups attempted to shelter long-term undocumented immigrants who had lived productively in this nation for decades from deportation and the negative effects of our chaotic immigration laws.

To live comfortably in a society, people have to feel that the structures of law and society are stable and just so that they know what is expected of them and that those expectations are fair and administered evenhandedly. When this is not the case, the result, ironically called "a police state," leaves people on edge, feeling constantly threatened by the very government that is supposed to keep them safe. This lack of basic safety, often visited on some classes of citizens and not others, is a great burden to those who experience it and should concern all of us, for it is incompatible with democracy.

Besides finding safety in society, relationships, and places, it is important for us to learn to find a sense of safety within ourselves. If we cannot calm ourselves and influence our own raging thoughts, we become our own enemies, especially in times of trauma or other difficulties. Among many ways to gain these skills is to practice meditation.

A common way to start a guided meditation is for a leader to invite participants to travel, in their imaginations, to a place where they feel safe and happy. At the end of such a meditation, people will report having "gone" to a beach or other natural spot, to a certain place in their childhood home, or to a place in their current home. Some go to the sanctuary of their religious home or a sanctuary they have visited. These are places where they have felt physically secure, psychologically safe, and in control of the situation.

Do you have such a safe place in your history or imagination? You can practice "going" there, noticing how it feels to be there, smelling its smells, hearing its sounds, and relaxing into its landscape. A regular trip to our safe place can prepare us for finding a sense of safety and control when our lives become anxious or chaotic. If you have to wait for the doctor's callback or the teenager's late arrival, it is so much nicer to be able to do so at the beach.

Just as wild animals increasingly need places set aside for them to simply live their lives in this crowded world, so we need places where we feel safe, people we feel safe with, the safety of justly managed civil society, and the ability to find a quiet place in our own minds and hearts. We need our sanctuaries.

Activities and Questions

1. Do you have a safe place to go to in your history or imagination? What makes that place feel safe?

2. Who do you feel safe with, and how did that sense of safety develop? (When you share in the group about this, remember that you should focus on yourself, even if you are talking about your relationship with another person.)

3. Think about a time when someone created a sense of safety for you or when you did this for someone else.

4. Do you have a sanctuary that you frequent, be it a religious building, a place in nature, or some other place? Describe it, especially the parts that are most meaningful to you.

5. Harold H. Bloomfield, in his book *How to Be Safe in This Increasingly Unsafe World* suggests, "Sit quietly and breathe deeply until you feel completely calm. Vividly picture a real-life experience that made you feel safe. Or imagine a strong sense of safety.

    When the picture is clear, come up with a 'sensory signal,' such as pressing your thumb and index finger together. If you repeat the exercise frequently, you will be able to elicit the feeling of safety every time you use your anchor touch."

    Try this exercise and describe to the group how it worked for you.

Thinking about the Words of the Day

Before coming to the gathering, think about some of the safe places in your life: buildings, rooms, natural areas, relationships, or activities that bring you a deep sense of safety. Be prepared to share a few words or phrases about several such places. The prompt for the Words of the Day activity will be to complete this sentence: "My safe place is/is like . . ."

GATHERING

Words of the Day

My safe place is/is like . . .

Chalice Lighting

We light this chalice [candle, lamp, etc.] to shine on our time together. In its light we celebrate the relationships and understanding we are creating in this place and time. May our sharing be deep. [Light the chalice.]

The Basket

Responsive Reading

Leader: The words we share . . .

Response: *come from our hearts, our minds, our lives.*

Leader: The feelings we express . . .

Response: *are real, important, and a part of the human heritage we all share.*

Leader: The ties we create in this community . . .

Response: *remind us of the web of creation, of which we are a part.*

On Our Hearts   10 minutes

Silence   3 minutes

Shared Readings

If I could keep my innermost Me
Fearless, aloof and free
Of the least breath of love or hate,
And not disconsolate
At the sick load of sorrow laid on men;
If I could keep a sanctuary there
Free even of prayer,
If I could do this, then,
With quiet candor as I grew more wise
I could look even at God with grave forgiving eyes.
　—Sara Teasdale

My first sanctuary was my family.
　—Christopher Jamison

The first step to creating an atmosphere of trust is setting boundaries. People need to know where they stand in order to feel safe enough to trust.
　—David Stark and Betty Veldman Wieland

I will know the place. It is quiet there. . . . It is the place of my beginning; it is the place of my ending; it is the place where I am whole. It is worth the journey. . . . It is my true self.
　—Christin Lore Weber

For me the door to the woods is the door to the temple.
　—Mary Oliver

We need to be known. This knowledge of being known we call love.
　—Alan Jones

Oh, the comfort—the inexpressible comfort of feeling safe with a person—having neither to weigh thoughts nor measure words, but pouring them all right out, just as they are, chaff and grain together; certain that a faithful hand will take and sift them, keep what is worth keeping, and then with the breath of kindness blow the rest away.

—Dinah Maria Mulock Craik

Sharing   60 minutes

Closing Circle

Extinguishing the Chalice

We extinguish this flame, and we remember the warmth of our community, the light of our wisdom, the generosity of our sharing. We keep these in our heart until we meet again. [Extinguish the chalice.]

Song/Silence

Announcements

THREE

Going Somewhere?

~

BEFORE YOU GATHER

And the world cannot be discovered by a journey of miles, no matter how long, but only by a spiritual journey, a journey of one inch, very arduous and humbling and joyful, by which we arrive at the ground at our feet, and learn to be at home.
　　—Wendell Berry

We have not even to risk the adventure alone; for the heroes of all time have gone before us; the labyrinth is thoroughly known; we have only to follow the thread of the hero-path. And where we had thought to find an abomination, we shall find a god; where we had thought to slay another, we shall slay ourselves; where we had thought to travel outward, we shall come to the center of our own existence; where we had thought to be alone, we shall be with all the world.
　　—Joseph Campbell

Not all those who wander are lost.
　　—J.R.R. Tolkien

The voyage into the self is long and dark and full of peril, but I believe that it is a voyage that all of us will have to make before we are through. Either we climb down into the abyss willingly with our eyes open, or we risk falling into it with our eyes closed . . . if we search ourselves deeply enough, we will begin to see at last who we really are, we will begin to see, very dimly at first, our own true faces.

—Frederick Buechner

Consider This

Been somewhere lately? When a question like that is asked, what it really means is, "Have you been somewhere *else* lately?" And the answer for most of us is, "Yes!" Between travel for business and travel for pleasure and family, Americans spend more than $2 trillion a year going somewhere else. The freedom and ability to travel are important to us. We like a change of scene; we have responsibilities elsewhere; we love to see new things and visit interesting places. Travel is enriching, we say, and vacations are best taken, if possible, away from home. We aren't alone in this. Literature from nearly the dawn of time tells us that trips and journeys make some of the best stories, and those stories still resonate with us today. Going elsewhere often brings good things into our lives.

The current mania for travel is not an unmitigated good, however. Science broadcaster and environmental activist David Suzuki estimates that aviation accounts for 4–9 percent of emissions associated with climate change, and that percentage is increasing as air travel increases and as other sectors curb emissions. When you take that family vacation in your car, you add twenty-four pounds of climate change gases to the atmosphere for every gallon of gas you use, according to the Union of Concerned Scientists. Five pounds comes from extraction, refinement, and delivery of the gas to the pump and a whopping nineteen pounds comes out of your car's tailpipe. Going somewhere has a big cost, not only to you but to the world.

A recurring (though not universal) teaching of human spiritual thinking is that travel is a distraction. *The Rule of Saint Benedict*, which is followed in Benedictine monastic communities, values "place" and encourages the disciplines of care, appreciation, and stability that allow monks to stay in place. Meanwhile, in Eastern spirituality, the *Tao Te Ching* makes reference to an ideal community in which the inhabitants of a well-governed country are so content with their homes and families that they have little interest in travel.

English author G. K. Chesterton opens his 1922 book *What I Saw in America* by commenting that travel narrows the mind, a heresy in his day as well as ours. He elaborates that travel "ought to combine amusement with instruction; but most travellers are so much amused that they refuse to be instructed." He also comments that it might be easier to feel the truth of human fellowship at a distance than when one is taken aback by differences in culture and mores. And those unfortunate enough to have spent much time at airline counters during a storm know that disruptions in travel can bring out the worst in our fellow human beings.

With those cautions in mind, let us consider what we're doing when we go somewhere. We take business trips, vacation trips, trips to visit or care for family and friends. The quintessential business trip involves flying somewhere on an airplane, checking into a nearby hotel, gathering in a windowless hotel meeting room with others who have flown in from other places, getting the work done, returning to the airport, and flying home. With luck, you'll be treated to a meal of local cuisine, but really, you could have been . . . anywhere. Many family trips involve a similar focus on people we already know, a place that is already explored, and a task that needs doing. These are all worthy movements from place to place, but what makes them important isn't the going somewhere.

We take sightseeing trips to see new and interesting places, to take pictures of those places, and to get bragging rights. This is a very diverting activity, but the very word *sightsee*—to see sights—suggests that it lacks depth. This is the activity about which Chesterton complained that we are so amused that we refuse to be instructed. Sightseeing is a combination of entertainment and refreshment.

We take vacation trips, often to places like beaches and mountain campgrounds, where we can simply rest and unwind, away from the house that needs painting, the yard that has become just too familiar, or the community activities that always beckon. Trips have their cost, both to us and to our world, and they have their benefits. But our lives will be richer if we also consider taking some journeys and perhaps even a pilgrimage.

A mere trip takes us somewhere else, but a journey changes us, and sometimes without taking us anyplace. We can take a journey to experience a new culture, to test ourselves in nature, or to live in a new way, but we can also take a journey into our own selves that does not involve physical travel. Going to college is a journey of growth for many people, even if they continue to live in their childhood home. Journeys are not always taken voluntarily, and the mythology of journeys, of which there is a great deal, suggests that the hero (not necessarily the savior, but the one about to experience transformation) often refuses the journey at first. In the Bible, Jonah is the archetype of the refuser: Asked by God to go and preach to the people of Nineveh, a dangerous assignment, Jonah promptly sets sail in the opposite direction.

Healing from a medical crisis often feels like an unchosen journey that we would have refused if we could, but that can be a fruitful period of growth in our lives nonetheless. A relationship change or a significant death can catapult us on a most uncomfortable journey, but if we are lucky we will find that we have changed for the better at its end. Even when we set off on a journey with willing excitement, it often has unexpected and unchosen twists and turns. What makes a journey, whether or not it involves travel, is psychological movement: insight, growth, a new direction for our lives.

Journeys, both of the travel and non-travel type, tend to have similar features. They have a beginning, sometimes referred to as a call, in which ordinary life is interrupted by an urgent new necessity or possibility. Then, sometimes after a refusal and a call that won't go away, comes the descent—the out-of-control second thoughts that have us asking, "What have I gotten myself into?" Jonah's ship, traveling in the wrong direction, encounters a storm that threatens everyone's safety. When Jonah confesses to the sailors that his disobedience is the cause of the storm, he gets thrown overboard and swallowed by a great sea beast. Time in the belly of the beast is also a part of a journey and time to confront ourselves and our choices. It is also a time to meet teachers and companions and experience the tribulations and learnings that bring transformation.

Finally, a journey involves a return to ordinary life, but we are changed, and ready, perhaps, for the next journey. Literature, from *The Iliad* to *The Lord of the Rings*, is replete with journeys that fit this pattern. But our own lives fit it as well. The phone rings; someone we love has been in an accident and we must go to their bedside. We turn off the stove, wonder if this is really happening, and brave the roads, the emergency unit, the medical lingo. We find those who can help us, we meet other loved ones who wait. We sit in a stew of anxiety, memory, and hope and find, perhaps, a peace we had not known before. Finally there is news. She will be all right. We should go home and rest. We walk out the doors, into the dawn, feeling somehow changed.

You can start out to take a trip and end up on a journey. The person who goes to visit aging parents and decides that he must help them move to assisted living turns a trip for himself into a journey for all three: for his parents, who must acknowledge their increasing dependence and frailty, and for their son, who finds himself taking on a new role with his parents and, sometimes, with his siblings. It's hard in lots of ways—not only in carrying boxes but in finding compassion in his heart for the different members of his family. He returns home new.

Some people think of our lives as a journey from birth to death. Thomas Merton, the mid-twentieth-century Catholic monk who traveled widely in both body and spirit, writes in his book *The*

Asian Journal of Thomas Merton, "Our real journey in life is interior: it is a matter of growth, deepening, and of an ever greater surrender to the creative action of love and grace in our hearts."

Spiritual journeys do not always fit the hero model, and sometimes more resemble the walkabout. A walkabout is a special kind of journey honored by the native people of Australia. It requires making a decision to take a first step, and a conscious and intentional movement (inwardly, outwardly, or both) in the direction of a longing or calling, with an openness to the actual experience, and a minimal attachment to expectations and results. Or as Interfaith minister Ken Seier puts it, "Walkabout is where you walk out into the desert until you find yourself." It's not as linear or neat as a Western-style hero's journey, but the West has its desert wandering stories too. The people of Israel wandered in the desert for forty years, throwing off the taint of their slavery, learning to govern themselves and trust God. A journey into the desert is a time-honored spiritual path, especially for persons of the Abrahamic traditions. The desert is the place you go, not to get someplace or to take on a certain task, but just to be, and in that being, to hear God speak—through dreams, visiting angels, or with a still, small voice in your heart.

Another type of travel is a pilgrimage. This is an intentional journey to a sacred place for the purpose of spiritual growth or fulfillment. The *haj*, the pilgrimage to Mecca required once in a lifetime of all Muslims who can manage it, is the classic pilgrimage. So is the *Camino de Santiago* in Spain, an old pilgrimage route that has recently become popular again. It is five hundred miles long and sprinkled with hostels and services for walkers; the journey, say those who take it, is both very physical (complete with blisters and exhaustion) and spiritual. In New Mexico, on Good Friday, Catholics of all ethnicities, plus many other religious and even non-religious people, walk from various places in the state to the Hispanic chapel in the town of Chimayo, which has long been thought of as a special place of healing. Some people walk for several weeks, others just for a day. Some walk on two legs, some use wheelchairs or crutches, and some have even crawled. So many people travel this road that police patrol the road to keep the walkers on the shoulder safe, and non-walkers set up rest and refreshment stations. The Good Friday walk to Chimayo is an experience best appreciated by extroverts. Those who appreciate quietness walk to this holy place on other days or take Good Friday walks to less-frequented sites.

Religious liberals don't always respond positively to the idea of a pilgrimage to a special, sacred space because many of us believe that the sacred is everywhere. "The great lesson . . . [is] that the sacred is *in* the ordinary, that it is to be found in one's daily life, in one's neighbors, friends, and family, in one's back yard," writes Abraham Maslow in his book *The Farther Reaches of Human Nature*. Maslow was one of the first psychologists of wellness and personal growth. His insight belongs squarely in those spiritual traditions that are somewhat suspicious of "going places." However it is also true that many people who feel that every place is sacred also experience sacredness more easily in some places than others. Long vistas, the sound of water, and the trials and prayers of one's fellow pilgrims help some move into a deeper, more spiritual space—and most of us need all the help we can get to stay motivated on our spiritual journey. We can affirm that the whole world is holy and still go on a pilgrimage to a place that seems especially holy to us. Hopefully the journey will prepare us to be receptive to whatever we experience when we arrive.

Whether we travel to the other half of the world or go on a journey of therapy exploring our personality, we eventually come home, return to ordinary life, go on with the new normal. It is then that we can judge the journey, asking what we have learned and how we have grown. We ask ourselves what seems different at home after this journey and notice how our responses to others have changed. Sometimes the fruits of a journey take several seasons to show themselves, and there will be times when we realize that we took only photos and left only footprints, and that is okay, too.

Activities and Questions

1. Think back on a voluntary journey you have taken. In what ways were you changed by the journey?

2. Think about a journey that was thrust upon you. What learning or insight did you discover at the end of the journey?

3. Think about a spiritual or interior journey you have taken. What have you discovered about yourself?

4. Treat yourself to a visual journey on the Internet: Watch the two-minute YouTube video "The Time Walker" by Sho Tsukikawa. Let it remind you of the journeys you have taken and what you learned from them.

5. If you have gone on a formal or informal pilgrimage, consider what that event has meant to you.

6. Watch the full-length movie *The Way*, starring Martin Sheen. Also consider reading *The Alchemist* by Paulo Coelho and *The Unlikely Pilgrimage of Harold Fry* by Rachel Joyce. Do these resources help you think about your life? In what way?

7. Sometimes a quotation and a piece of art seem to be intertwined, although they were not created together. One such pairing is a quotation from novelist Haruki Murakami and the painting *Anthropomorphic Chest of Drawers* by Salvador Dali. Murakami writes, "We have rooms in ourselves. Most of them we have not visited yet. Forgotten rooms. From time to time we can find the passage. We find strange things . . . they belong to us, but it is the first time we have found them." Both artists are probing the inner journey. What hidden rooms in yourself have you glimpsed or sensed the presence of?

Thinking about the Words of the Day

Before coming to the gathering, think of a few words, phrases, or metaphors that describe a journey or pilgrimage. The prompt for the Words of the Day activity will be to complete this sentence: "My journey is . . ."

GATHERING

Words of the Day

My journey is . . .

Chalice Lighting

We light this chalice [candle, lamp, etc.] to shine on our time together. In its light we celebrate the relationships and understanding we are creating in this place and time. May our sharing be deep. [Light chalice.]

The Basket

Responsive Reading

Leader: The words we share . . .

Response: *come from our hearts, our minds, our lives.*

Leader: The feelings we express . . .

Response: *are real, important, and a part of the human heritage we all share.*

Leader: The ties we create in this community . . .

Response: *remind us of the web of creation, of which we are a part.*

On Our Hearts   10 minutes

Silence   3 minutes

Shared Readings

Unlike mere travel, a pilgrimage is a journey into the landscape of the soul.
   —Vivienne Hull

Take nothing
for your journey.
Only your longing,
your unknowing,
your insufficiency.
   —Mary Vineyard

A holy restlessness is what prompts the pilgrimage of the spirit—a journey real or metaphorical that calls us away from what we have grown to think of as our home in order to discover a deeper sense of being at home with our human nature.
   —Sarah York

Each day is a journey, and the journey itself home.
   — Matsuo Basho

Not I, not any one else can travel that road for you,
You must travel it for yourself.
   —Walt Whitman

A labyrinth is a symbolic journey . . . but it is a map we can really walk on, blurring the difference between map and world.
   —Rebecca Solnit

We travel, some of us forever, to seek other states, other lives, other souls.
   —Anaïs Nin

I have arrived.
I am home.
    —Thich Nhat Hanh

Sharing   60 minutes

Closing Circle

Extinguishing the Chalice

We extinguish this flame, and we remember the warmth of our community, the light of our wisdom, the generosity of our sharing. We keep these in our hearts until we meet again. [Extinguish the chalice.]

Song/Silence

Announcements

FOUR

Soul

~

BEFORE YOU GATHER

The only metaphor I know that reflects the soul's essence while honoring its mystery: the soul is like a wild animal. Like a wild animal, the soul is tough, resilient, resourceful, savvy, and self-sufficient: it knows how to survive in hard places. . . . Yet despite its toughness, the soul is also shy. Just like a wild animal, it seeks safety in the dense underbrush, especially when other people are around. If we want to see a wild animal, we know that the last thing we should do is go crashing through the woods yelling for it to come out. But if we will walk quietly into the woods, sit patiently at the base of a tree, breathe with the earth, and fade into our surroundings, the wild creature we seek might put in an appearance. We may see it only briefly and only out of the corner of an eye—but the sight is a gift we will always treasure as an end in itself.

—Parker J. Palmer

How do I write about the making of a soul. . . . As we shall see, human beings are not made overnight. Nor, indeed, is the process ever finished. The word "soul" is a metaphor for this process of transformation.

—Alan Jones

At the center of our being is a point of nothingness which is untouched by sin and by illusion, a point of pure truth, a point or spark which belongs entirely to God . . .
—Thomas Merton

Consider This

On an elementary school playground years ago, a little girl once told her friends, with an air of authority, that the soul is like a heart with wings, and it flies away from our body after we die. She'd learned that in Sunday school and even seen a picture. She had also heard that the soul is the part of us that holds our sins, that it gets dirty and heavy and soiled when we are willful, naughty, or bad. She told the other girls that Jesus forgives our sins and that cleans up our soul, but just like when you erase a paper and leave a smudge, the soul is a little stained, even with forgiveness, so it is better to be perfect in the first place.

Although that young theologian had been introduced to these ideas (and the picture) in a Catholic church, most adult Catholics would cringe to hear this theology, which is not at all the official teaching of the church. But the children hearing the story on the playground didn't know that. And there is something about the smudged-up paper that so accorded with their school experience of hardly ever being perfect, or even, for some, hardly ever being good enough, that made the story compelling and worrisome. Even the listener who suspected that her atheist parents would reject this belief worried just a little, and she closed the book on that strange word, *soul*.

Later in her life, she found her childhood atheism relaxing and she became more willing to wonder, not only about science and nature and the things that can be seen and reasoned over but also about old words and ideas like *spirit, worship, God, salvation, prayer,* and *soul,* which so many people through ages and cultures have found so valuable. She decided that she was not willing to let her bad experience with these words, and all the foolish ways they are used, keep her from finding her own definitions for them and to use them in her own way. She reasoned that they are all powerful words that have no real equivalents in less religious language, and they are too valuable to let playground definitions prevail.

Eventually, she came to think of soul as the part of each of us that is most precious, not most sullied, the part that connects us to others and to the universe, to God and Goddess and Spirit and Nature. She pictured the essence of her own life as something like an hourglass: the wide top and bottom reach into the world, and that narrow place in the middle is where the depth of her being meets the depth of the world. She liked what the poet Mary Oliver once said in *Amicus Journal*, "This is the first, wildest, and wisest thing I know, that the soul exists, and that it is built entirely out of attentiveness." And she started to value paying attention. She resonated with Unitarian minister A. Powell Davies, who said, "Life is just a chance to grow a soul." And she began to value her own growth, not only as good for her but as good for the whole world.

Process theologian Alfred North Whitehead defines the soul as the "organ of novelty" in his book *Process and Reality*. He uses the word *soul* to identify the creative and transformative powers of imagination that renew and revivify all things. He felt that those creative and transformative sources were the processes of the divine. By also speaking of them as *soul*, he connected our inner lives and intimate selves with what he thought was ultimate in the universe.

A very different perspective on this elusive word comes to us from African-American culture, which speaks informally of soul not as a thing but as a quality that partakes deeply of black culture. In African-American vernacular, you don't say that something *is* a soul, you say that something's *got* soul. Soul food is the traditional food of Southern blacks, and a meal of soul food is not just a feast for the taste buds and stomach but a connection to a proud, survivor people who were impoverished but who nonetheless cooked creatively and frugally with what they had. To eat soul food is not only to nourish the body but to partake of values and community and ethos and thereby to nourish the heart and spirit.

The religious community has not managed to incorporate this definition of soul into its thinking, but the art community has. Artists sometimes speak of a work having soul; more often a piece of music or a specific performance is deemed soulful, which is to say, expressive of deep emotion or meaning and nourishing to the listener in a special way. In the art world also, soul is not a thing but a quality, a quality of depth or connection that is achieved in the creative process when it has reached deeply into the truths of life.

It's a useful category for other parts of life. A wedding ceremony, for instance, is, at its best, a soulful experience. Love is present, two become one, a community of friends and family offers their blessings. The setting has been specially prepared with decorations, music, food, and flowers. Those present are reminded not only of their relationship to the happy couple and family but of their own experiences of love and vows of faithfulness. A wonderful wedding is a spiritual experience for all who take part.

If you've been to enough weddings (or if you read the advice columnists), you know that not all weddings have soul. Some get bogged down in the color of napkins or the value of gifts or in family dysfunction or bridal neediness. Couples are often too stressed out from planning and managing to experience the soul qualities of their own weddings. If they don't even have the language to think about this quality, it is likely to slip away from them.

The Pueblo Indians, who do have language for this quality of soulfulness, are more intentional about their ceremonies. They are an inherently hospitable people and believe that they are doing their ceremonies for the world and that, therefore, the world should be invited. But their hospitality is regularly strained by tourists. A tourist is, almost by definition, someone who observes a foreign event or surveys a foreign scene with curiosity but without soul. This is because soul requires knowledge, connection, and time. Tourists don't usually have those things. And to make up for their lack, they want to take pictures.

To some Native Americans, taking pictures of people, especially in a ceremonial setting, takes away soul—not because of any superstition about pictures but because someone who is taking pictures isn't fully participating in the event. They are focusing on the technology of the camera and on the ego rush of posting to Facebook or the future pleasure of looking at pictures. So the Pueblo people forbid cameras at their ceremonies. And many tourists, deprived of their cameras, have discovered themselves strangely moved by the dances and ceremonies and vivid memories of being pulled into something new.

The cultivation of soul or soulfulness in our own lives is not a straight-line proposition. Soul has its power and integrity, and its development can be fostered, but not forced.

Soul is cultivated by appreciating beauty in all of its forms; by remembering and cherishing all that moves us; by noting our yearnings, wounds, and healings; by sympathizing with other human beings and their yearnings, wounds, and healings. Soul is cultivated by working with others for common goals and enjoying the community that results. Soul grows, in other words, when we are stretched by our lives. And while soulfulness is something that we can desire, appreciate, and tend, it develops in its own way and time. We can play our part by living in ways that stretch and deepen our lives.

No doubt you've known people who you might consider as having soul. No doubt you have attended events or appreciated works of art that seemed soulful. If soulfulness is a quality that you'd like to develop in yourself, you can pay attention to your deep connections and great joys and give them the space to grow. You can cherish the opportunities for growth that come your way, even when they are painful or inconvenient. You can put yourself in the way of experiences that make you an attentive pilgrim, rather than a tourist, on life's great road.

We grow our souls when we ask ourselves to consider the wider consequences of our decisions and ways of life. One lovely expression of a soulful way of life is the idea, which comes from the Iroquois people, that we should consider how a proposal will affect not just people alive today but those who will be affected in the future, up to the seventh generation. Only the wise can manage to care about what will happen in 150 years.

As to the soul you have (if you think you have one)—that which is deeply you and transcends your death—perhaps these deep and wise ways of living that we call soulful will grow that mystical organ as well, bringing light to the universe even beyond the seventh generation!

Activities and Questions

1. How would you describe soul? How would you describe your soul?

2. What might you add to your life to cultivate your soul? What conditions help you cultivate your soul? Think of a few spiritual disciplines that could aid you.

3. What piece of music or art would you call soulful?

4. Who would you call a soulful person? What qualities does this person have?

5. How much silence is in your life to encourage the shy soul to come forth?

6. Read the delightful children's book *Play With Me* by Marie Hall Ets. It tells of a young child wishing to play with the shy animals in the woods. You can find it in your public library or find a reading of the book on YouTube.

Thinking about the Words of the Day

Before coming to the gathering, think of a few words, phrases, or metaphors that describe a soul, or your soul in particular. The prompt for the Words of the Day activity will be to complete this sentence: "My soul is/is like . . ."

GATHERING

Words of the Day

My soul is/is like . . .

Chalice Lighting

We light this chalice [candle, lamp, etc.] to shine on our time together. In its light we celebrate the relationships and understanding we are creating in this place and time. May our sharing be deep. [Light chalice.]

The Basket

Responsive Reading

Leader: The words we share . . .

Response: *come from our hearts, our minds, our lives.*

Leader: The feelings we express . . .

Response: *are real, important, and a part of the human heritage we all share.*

Leader: The ties we create in this community . . .

Response: *remind us of the web of creation, of which we are a part.*

On Our Hearts   10 minutes

Silence   3 minutes

Shared Readings

"Soul" is not a thing but a quality or a dimension of experiencing life and ourselves. It has to do with depth, value, relatedness, heart, and personal substance.

—Thomas Moore

Women need solitude in order to find again the true essence of themselves: that firm strand which will be the indispensable center of a whole web of human relationships. She must find that inner stillness which Charles Morgan describes as "the stilling of the soul within the activities of the mind and body so that it might be still as the axis of a revolving wheel is still."

—Anne Morrow Lindbergh

Philosophers haggle about what to call this core of our humanity, but I am no stickler for precision. Thomas Merton called it true self. Buddhists call it original nature or big self. Quakers call it the inner teacher or the inner light. Hasidic Jews call it a spark of the divine. Humanists call it identity and integrity. In popular parlance, people often call it soul.

—Parker J. Palmer

Sometimes I go about pitying myself, and all along my soul is being blown by great winds across the sky.

—Ojibway saying

Still, there is something in the human spirit that requires silence as the body needs food and oxygen.

—Marc De Souza

Put your ear down close to your soul and listen hard.

—Anne Sexton

There is a spectacle grander than the sea, and that is the sky; there is a spectacle grander than the sky, and it is the interior of the soul.
—Victor Hugo

Sharing   60 minutes

Closing Circle

Extinguishing the Chalice

We extinguish this flame, and we remember the warmth of our community, the light of our wisdom, the generosity of our sharing. We keep these in our heart until we meet again. [Extinguish the chalice.]

Song/Silence

Announcements

FIVE

Security, Serenity, Peace of Mind

∾

BEFORE YOU GATHER

For peace of mind resign as general manager of the universe.
—Larry Eisenberg

Set peace of mind as your highest goal. Organize your life around it this goal.
—Brian Tracy

So do not worry about tomorrow, for tomorrow will bring worries of its own. Today's trouble is enough for today.
—Matthew 6:34

It is possible to experience peace of mind even when chaos is going on all around me or in my body.
—Gerald G. Jampolsky

Consider This

Security is the feeling of being safe and in control. It's a nice feeling. It exists on a continuum. You can feel a little bit safe and in control or totally safe and in control. Everybody needs at least some security, and our search for security and control begins soon after birth, when we discover that our cry will bring us someone to attend to our needs. Take somebody's sense of security and control away from them and they are likely to feel very stressed. We need a sense of security to be happy, productive, and creative.

Security is assisted but not created by material things and good planning. Indeed, complete security and total control over one's life can be influenced but never guaranteed. Billionaires die. You can eat right and exercise a lot and still have a heart attack at forty-eight. You can use every ounce of wisdom and self-discipline you have as you parent your kids, and they might still get in trouble. You can take every reasonable precaution and still get pregnant. Defensive drivers only lessen their chances of being in an accident. Careful, productive workers are sometimes fired. Armed citizens are regularly robbed and sometimes shot with their own guns. Running with the right crowd only helps you stay out of trouble. In short, there is no fortress so high as to keep out the bad guys, no lifestyle so healthy as to guarantee immortality. There is no security. We are not in control.

There are degrees of security, and some degree of security is appropriate and necessary. The fact that no fortress can keep the bad guys out does not mean that you might as well leave your door open and invite them in. There are plenty of precautions to take, just no guarantees that they will always work. It is sensible to lock up your house when you leave it. But if you're not willing to even open a window to let the fresh air in, your need for security has started to make life miserable. Parents want to keep their children safe. But if they are so nervous about the safety of their children that they will not let them walk to school with the other children or ever be out of their sight in a public place, how will the children grow up and develop independence? Everyone wants to keep their jewelry and silver safe. But if that means keeping it in a vault, unused, you might as well just sell it.

An all-out quest for security can severely limit our lives. Even worse, it can drain us of compassion for others and ourselves when the inevitable bad things do happen. If we tell ourselves that we are in control of our lives and, because of our goodness and diligence, will never get sick or lose our jobs, it will be hard for us to be compassionate to someone who has had this happen. And when it happens to us, we will not only have to cope with misfortune but we will also have to do the hard work of adopting a more realistic view of life at the same time.

Security is best understood as an illusion, even as we take prudent steps to keep ourselves as safe as possible. The quest for inappropriate amounts of security in our lives damages us and damages others. We live best if we learn to live with the knowledge that we are not in control.

Serenity is something else entirely. To be serene is to be calm, unruffled, unconflicted, and peaceful. It is a state of mind rather than a matter of safety; it is possible (although possibly not wise) to be serene in the face of danger or difficulty. Countless books have been written, lectures given, and sermons preached on how to attain the ellusive state of serenity. Unitarian minister of the 1950s A. Powell Davies once preached about receiving an advertisement promising serenity for a dollar a year:

> It seemed like a bargain. In case I did not have a dollar, the agency would promptly send me a little cardboard bank in which I could save a dollar up a dime at a time. Perhaps it was the thoughtfulness of this arrangement that predisposed me to read the entire communication. At any rate, I read it. And this is what I found: that I can know exactly what to do in every situation, and how to do it perfectly, for God in the midst of me will be my intelligence. That is to say, He will if I send this institution a dollar a year.

We all know that it can't possibly be that easy and we can smell a scam even over the distance of years. But Davies goes on to point out that a calm and unruffled attitude toward all things is not necessarily appropriate. There are things that are worth getting riled up, upset, and anxious over.

No one was a better example of this than Davies himself, an enormously powerful preacher of the All Souls Unitarian Church in Washington, D.C. He was so popular that people gathered by the hundreds in satellite locations in suburban elementary school cafeterias to listen to his preaching by primitive phone hook-up because his church downtown was full. His sermons were so highly regarded that they were excerpted in the *Washington Post* on Monday mornings. Davies could have rested on his laurels and cultivated peacefulness and serenity. But he was so disturbed by Senator Joseph McCarthy's false and unjust accusations of communism, so convinced that this man and his antics were a danger to democracy, that he took the senator on. He was one of the first to do so and suffered the consequences of being labeled a communist, but he went on fighting. No serenity here. His courage paved the way for others to begin to fight back against demagoguery. McCarthy was defeated in the end, and Davies died at the age of fifty-five. There is no security in life. Goodness or worth does not guarantee anything. And serenity, as attractive as it can be, is not an unmitigated good; it can cause us to be complacent about dangers and injustices.

The phrase *peace of mind* describes another goal, perhaps more worthy, as it allows for both contentment and activism. Peace of mind doesn't come from sending dimes to scam artists, finding the perfect form of meditation, or avoiding the slings and arrows of outrageous fortune. Peace of mind comes from living a real life and making peace with its conflicts.

Peace of mind, unlike security, which is impossible, and serenity, which can lead us astray, should be our focus. It is not easy to attain but worth the effort. How to begin? Researchers at Duke University interviewed people about characteristics that give them peace of mind. The study concluded that peace of mind is not something you have or don't have, like flipping a switch, but it is something you have to a greater or lesser degree. Here are some characteristics of people who seem to have attained a greater degree of peace of mind:

- They are generally trusting. They don't seem to have much hostility or suspicion. This doesn't mean wide-eyed gullibility. It means that people who enjoy peace of mind don't go looking for trouble and they assume that people are well-intentioned, competent, and good unless faced with contrary evidence.

- They live in the present and find happiness and satisfaction in the moment. Living on memories while in the prime of life doesn't make for peace of mind; we are built to strive more than to remember. Nor does a lifestyle that postpones all happiness until some later date make for peace of mind, for we know, in our heart of hearts, that that date may not come.

- They don't waste energy fighting conditions that cannot be changed. Peace of mind is not a matter of never exerting ourselves for a better future but of choosing our battles wisely and not expending energy pointlessly. Peace of mind is the result of accepting what you can't change and working to change what you can. Discerning one from the other is not always easy and sometimes requires some experimentation.

- They are not in denial about life's problems. Even if the conscious mind can sometimes be fooled, the unconscious mind cannot, and peace of mind is a holistic condition. It involves accepting appropriate responsibility for our lives and circumstances and realistic understanding that life is never completely secure. Although feeling sorry for oneself is a natural response to life's misfortunes, people who enjoy peace of mind move out of that unpleasant mindset and get to work.

- They know how to reach out to others, especially in times of stress. Whether naturally introverted or extroverted, they don't hide away when faced with adversity; they join with others, ask for help, and talk through their problems. They also reach out to others to give support and maintain connections when others are in painful situations. Introverts will probably do this one-on-one while extroverts are more likely to choose group settings, but peace of mind is not an individual sport. Maintaining our connections in times of difficulty offers us solace and practical support and keeps us from feeling personally picked on by a hostile universe. Wherever we turn, we will find others who have been through what we are going through; we can benefit from their knowledge and find comfort in community. This community is one of the major ways religious groups, whatever their theology, bring peace of mind to their members.

- They cultivate basic values. They keep commitments, speak the truth in love, generally obey the law, and thoughtfully consider the impact of their social roles. In short, they do the right things and can rest in the comforting knowledge that they are good people. They have peace of mind because their conscience does not bother them.

- Finally, they are realistic and they adjust to human limitations. This means they strike a balance between what they'd like to think of themselves and what they can actually accomplish. Peace of mind comes from knowing ourselves and living with ourselves the way we are. No one is so miserable as the person who won't be happy unless he attains the presidency, makes a million dollars, or writes the great American novel. We have to be realistic and enjoy our lives whether or not we attain our highest goals.

Peace of mind is not something that we ever attain once and for all. Over a lifetime of practice, we attain it and lose it in degrees. It is worth the pursuit. Being trusting and trustworthy, realistic and dependable, comfortably connected to others, able to live happily in the present, and willing to do the right thing will enhance our lives and lay the groundwork for peace of mind. Although we are never secure and ought not to be always serene, pursuing peace of mind helps us become more comfortable as we live well and responsibly in the world.

Activities and Questions

1. Think of a time when you let go of an expectation about yourself, let go of driving yourself, and settled into peace.

2. Think of something in your life that is causing you great anxiety. What are you doing to achieve peace of mind in spite of this?

3. On a scale of 1–10, how would you rate yourself on your need to be in control? What consequences does this have? Do you have strategies to help you deal with this?

4. Look over the following characteristics of people who have peace of mind. Choose one or two that you feel you have and mark these with *. Next, choose one or two that are a challenge for you and mark them with **. Think about how you might share this with the group.

   trusting
   living in the present
   accepting what you can't change
   avoiding denial
   connecting with others in time of stress

accepting responsibility

living an honorable life

striking a balance between what you want to do and what you
actually can do

Thinking about the Words of the Day

Look at the characteristics listed above that support peace of mind.
Think of some recent experiences when you were aware of one of
these characteristics in your life. The prompt for the Words of the
Day activity will be to complete this sentence: "I practice/experi-
ence peace of mind when I . . ."

GATHERING

Words of the Day

I practice/experience peace of mind when I . . .

Chalice Lighting

We light this chalice [candle, lamp, etc.] to shine on our time together. In its light we celebrate the relationships and understanding we are creating in this place and time. May our sharing be deep. [Light chalice.]

The Basket

Responsive Reading

Leader: The words we share . . .

Response: *come from our hearts, our minds, our lives.*

Leader: The feelings we express . . .

Response: *are real, important, and a part of the human heritage we all share.*

Leader: The ties we create in this community . . .

Response: *remind us of the web of creation, of which we are a part.*

On Our Hearts   10 minutes

Silence   3 minutes

Shared Readings

God give us grace to accept with serenity the things that cannot be changed, courage to change the things that should be changed, and the wisdom to distinguish the one from the other.
    —Reinhold Niebuhr

When you reach out, others, in turn, will reach in to you. You will not be alone. It can be hard to hear this, especially when you are low, lost or lonely, but *you* have to reach out to others *first*, if you want people to reach for you. It starts with *you*.
    —Dee Shemma

Security is mostly a superstition. . . . Life is either a daring adventure or nothing.
    —Helen Keller

Once you surrender to the fact that you are unable to control the uncertainty, you will, at last, be able to breathe a sigh of relief.
    —Susan Jeffers

We all have circumstances in our lives that don't meet up to our plans and expectations.
    —Amy E. Spiegel

There are various reasons why people endure stress and can't seem to reach out for support. . . . There is no shame in seeking advice for something as potentially harmful as stress.
    —Richard D. Murphy

Do you see your life as a dance between trust and fear? When your trust level is high, are you more capable of handling a difficulty than you are when you're afraid?
    —Amy E. Dean

Sharing   60 minutes

Closing Circle

Extinguishing the Chalice

We extinguish this flame, and we remember the warmth of our community, the light of our wisdom, the generosity of our sharing. We keep these in our heart until we meet again. [Extinguish the chalice.]

Song/Silence

Announcements

SIX

Fair Is Fair

∾

BEFORE YOU GATHER

Nothing's fair in this world. You might as well get that straight right now.
  —Sue Monk Kidd

Where do I get my sense of what is fair and what is unfair?
  —Harold S. Kushner

Fairness isn't an objective truth. True fairness is a fluid *process* of blending different legacies of owing and deserving from the mix that each person brings to the relationship. But before partners can thoughtfully negotiate fairness, they both must sort out their inherited model of expectations for what they owe and deserve.
  —B. Janet Hibbs and Karen J. Getzen

Fairness and justice do not exist in nature; the sun and moon set and rise without justification.
  —Jason A. Junge

Consider This

Most people have at least one vivid childhood memory of feeling that something was unfair. It could be the realization that someone else was the teacher's pet, or an unequally divided treat, or a playground scuffle that was two against one. Some of us remember getting preferential treatment ourselves and feeling that that wasn't fair, or learning about a social condition that outraged our young hearts.

Fairness is hardwired into human beings, and not just humans either. Some of our simian cousins also have a keen eye for fairness and a sense of outrage when they feel unfairly treated. In an elegant experiment, researchers trained two monkeys to perform an identical task—hand a rock to a researcher. Upon completion of the task, the researcher gave a treat—either a cucumber, which monkeys like very much, or a grape, which they like even better. The two monkeys were put in adjacent cages so that they could see each other and each was asked to do the task. Upon completion, the researcher gave one monkey a piece of cucumber, while the second monkey got a grape. The first monkey realized right away that she was being shortchanged and let the researcher know about it in no uncertain terms.

A need for fairness is in our very genes. This is not surprising. Like monkeys, we are social animals. We must live together to survive. But without fairness as a part of that living together, society falls apart. People become demoralized, uninclined to trust others or make sacrifices for them. Without fairness we are either enslaved or alone.

Fairness is not something that we see in the natural world. The lion attacks the mother goat in labor, the blessing of rain falls on the good and bad alike, accidents happen. Humans resist this fact and have tried many ways to explain how the obvious unfairness of life is not really unfair. For instance:

- Many people from a variety of faiths believe that the source of what seems like unfairness in our lives is not unfairness, but a manifestation of justice for something their soul did or didn't do in a past life. The Hindus call this Karma and have complex doctrines surrounding it, but this belief occurs in many pagan faiths and one hears it said, playfully but with a serious undertone, even in secular society. Some people suffering through no obvious fault of their own find comfort in the idea that their situation is not unfair because of something hidden in a past life. Others suffer doubly, as they deal not only with misfortune, but with the shame of somehow having caused it.

- When things don't seem fair in this life, some varieties of Christianity teach they will be made fair by God in the afterlife. A particularly harsh version of Christianity (Calvinism) says that, since we are all born with a deep streak of sinfulness, all the bad things that happen to us in this life and the next are still "fair." More commonly, Christians teach that God is with us when bad things happen to us, and many Christians—and others, even those who don't believe in God—have an experience of God's comforting presence in extremely difficult times.

- The ancient Hebrews understood unfairness with the help of a doctrine called "Divine Earthly Retribution." That's the idea that if you do something bad, God will make sure you suffer right here and now, in this life, and if you are suffering, it is because you did something bad. The corollary is that if you are prospering, it is because you are being rewarded for being good. The Protestant work ethic is one version of this doctrine, and it has been a powerful former of culture, even though it doesn't take much observation to throw doubt on its claim. Even the ancient Hebrews were uncomfortable with this way of explaining how life is fair: Plenty of Psalms express lament that the wicked are getting away with murder and the entire book of Job in the Hebrew Bible is devoted to a story of a good man who suffered unjustly and demands of God to know why. The answer he gets is, "Just because." But the fact that God spoke to him at all is profoundly comforting to Job.

- Secularists, humanists, and atheists the world over have said bluntly that nature is blind and fairness is not a category that can be applied to what happens to us by chance. Most secularists believe that society and other people can and should help to mitigate suffering caused by various "acts of nature" such as storms, accidents, and disease, as well as create structures such as building codes and traffic laws to lessen the negative forces of pure chance.

Many people remember being taught one or more of these ways of dealing with the unfairness of life as children, and those lessons often stick with us throughout our lives and are powerful even when we have intellectually rejected them.

However we manage and explain the fairness of "life," we have to also manage the fairness of other people and the society in which we live. And that is harder. Because while it may be that life is not "supposed" to be fair, we do expect good people and good families and good governments to be fair. Even so, there are many ways for people and families and governments to be fair.

Monkeys don't waste any energy expecting life to be fair. If one monkey finds a grape and another finds a piece of cucumber, there may be a scuffle but there will be no outrage, no fist-shaking at God or nature. What they do expect is for *transactions* to be fair. They expect, as do children, as do all of us unless experience beats it out of us, that people will be fair. Fairness doesn't exist in nature. Fairness is created and expressed in societies. If we want to live in a fair society, we have to make it fair. But how?

First, we must consider justice, which is not exactly the same thing as fairness but is a specific kind of fairness. Justice is the fairness of governments and social structures that have the force of law. It is how laws apply to everyone, how officials treat different people, and how social good gets divided.

Fairness happens in families and between individuals, in informal social situations. It includes how families share a dessert, how co-workers divvy up work, how neighbors decide what to do about a tree on the property line.

Justice can be divided into two types: procedural and distributive. Procedural justice governs the process. Distributive justice tells us who is entitled to what products of society.

In some families, the rule when a treat must be divided between two children is that one child does the dividing and the other gets first pick of the resulting pieces. If the roles are alternated, this is a fair procedure, even though the result will often be that one child gets a larger piece. Procedural fairness in a store policy might require that everyone, even a senior citizen, is carded before purchasing alcohol. This feels absurd or even disrespectful to the senior, but it prevents clerks from playing favorites. Procedural fairness at the voting site means that the same identification is required of everyone (or no one) and that the same procedure is followed each time by two poll workers, one from each major party.

Research published in the *Journal of Experimental Criminology* shows that when people believe that they have been treated with procedural fairness, they will be better citizens and happier even with results that do not favor them.

Governments and especially businesses that want people to feel fairly treated have discovered that it is not enough to treat everybody the same. That might *be* fair, but it might not *feel* fair. For example, if people don't know the rules in advance, they are likely to be angry about a result that doesn't favor them—even if it was procedurally fair. If they are not treated respectfully, they will be unhappy with any result. If they think they have been singled out for enforcement while others got by, they will be angry even if they were in the wrong. Carefully trained law enforcement agents want the public to be fairly treated and, as much as possible, to *feel* fairly treated, so they have protocols to make this more likely. A "good cop" who stops you for speeding will be stopping everyone going over a certain speed (or every third person going over a certain speed or some other formula to ensure that no class of persons is singled out). If you get pulled over by a well-trained officer who understands how important procedural fairness is, you'll be treated respectfully and probably addressed as sir or ma'am. The officer will tell you why you were pulled over (so you won't wonder if you were singled out for a non-legal reason such as your race or age) and ask you if you know what the speed limit is and how fast you were going (to remind you that you know the rules and should have known how fast you were driving). That's good policing. Good policing makes happier citizens who are more likely to obey the law. Procedural justice is crucially important to good government.

Distributive justice, on the other hand, relates to who gets access to the resources that are created when people work together in societies. None of us would survive long or happily if we had nothing but our wits and our skin to survive with, so some kind of distributive justice is necessary for every society. Every society has rules of distributive justice that allow people to know what rightfully belongs to them. These rules tend to fall into four categories.

- "The strongest take whatever they want and the devil take the hindmost." So some would say about how to distribute the goods of society. Yet most people don't want to live in a society with this kind of rule because strength and the ability to take what you want usually are not the most highly valued traits in society.

- "We divide things equally." One cupcake, two kids? Each one gets half. A state must compensate a school district for educating children? A per capita amount is agreed on and all districts get the same. This is called equity and it is one kind of fairness. In simple situations it works well. But people are not usually simple and equity often does not seem "fair." If one child can enjoy an inexpensive supermarket cupcake while another has dietary needs that require a more expensive treat, then giving both children the same amount of money to buy a treat will seem cruel rather than fair.

- "We divide things so that everyone gets what they need for a decent life." Since people have different needs, the goods of society can be divided, not so that everyone gets the same, but so that everyone has an equal quality of life. If the two children sharing one cupcake are ages two and ten, it could be seen as fair to give the two-year-old a quarter of it and the ten-year-old three-quarters. Some children will learn to read perfectly well in a classroom of twenty students, but some will need individual help, so most states give school districts that have lots of special needs children more money. This could be termed *outcome equality*, and it is distinctly different from equity, which requires that everyone gets the same resources. Outcome equality is how most families work. The baby needs to go to the doctor, so there's no allowance this week. Mary's piano lessons may cost more than John's drawing paper, but the important thing is that each spouse has what they need to pursue a hobby. In human groups much larger than families and tribes, however, it becomes tricky to decide what people really need and how to make things fair.

- "Those who contribute the most get the most." This is called proportionate fairness. Those who work the hardest, the smartest, or the most productively make the biggest salaries. This is supposed to be the way capitalism works. One of the angsts of our time is that many people are realizing that our economic system has become rigged. These days many of the most highly compensated people in our nation are not the most productive ones but the very ones who have brought on market crashes, with all the suffering that has resulted from them. Conservative economics writer David Brooks called this "the perverse compensation schemes on Wall Street." Proportionate fairness, like outcome fairness, works well in small groups and families where work, skill, and contribution are easily agreed upon. But in larger systems, there are more hidden ways to manipulate outcomes so that fair is no longer fair. Who is to say that Wall Street executives are worth more than doctors, or that the work of a college professor is worth five times the work of a preschool teacher?

As we can see, rather than "fair is fair," fairness is actually pretty complicated. Any society that most of its people think is fair is going to have a combination of all three kinds of distributive fairness, with a critically important dollop of procedural fairness on top. It will also have an undercurrent of "the strongest take what they want"—especially in places the law does not reach.

Fairness is complicated, and often when our initial reaction to a situation causes us to declare "That's not fair!" with outrage, it is useful to ask ourselves which model of fairness we are applying and whether it is the most appropriate. Understanding that there are fundamentally different kinds of fairness will also help us to recognize why good people can sometimes differ about what is fair and can help us to communicate with those who disagree with us.

Activities and Questions

1. Do you have a vivid childhood memory around fairness? What is it and how do you think it shaped the rest of your life?

2. Do you remember what you were taught or believed over the years about what makes things fair and unfair? How did those beliefs shape your life?

3. Some say you must be fair to others as you are fair to yourself—a Golden Rule of fairness. Are you generally lenient with yourself but hard on others, or are you more likely to be hard on yourself but give others the benefit of the doubt? Where did that trait come from and what have you done to find balance?

4. Think of a time recently when your "fairness monitor" went off. Ask yourself why the situation didn't seem fair and by what model of fairness it might seem fair. If you share about this in the group, focus your sharing on yourself and your feelings, even if you need to explain the situation that you found unfair.

5. There are several kinds of fairness. Describe an experience in your life in which dividing equally seemed fair to you. Describe a time when you received more or less than others because "outcome fairness" was in play. Or describe a time when you benefited or were harmed by proportionate fairness.

Thinking about the Words of the Day

Before coming to the gathering, think of a few words, phrases, or metaphors that describe fairness. The prompt for the Words of the Day activity will be to complete this sentence: "It's not fair when ..."

GATHERING

Words of the Day

It's not fair when . . .

Chalice Lighting

We light this chalice [candle, lamp, etc.] to shine on our time together. In its light we celebrate the relationships and understanding we are creating in this place and time. May our sharing be deep. [Light chalice.]

The Basket

Responsive Reading

Leader: The words we share . . .

Response: *come from our hearts, our minds, our lives.*

Leader: The feelings we express . . .

Response: *are real, important, and a part of the human heritage we all share.*

Leader: The ties we create in this community . . .

Response: *remind us of the web of creation, of which we are a part.*

On Our Hearts   10 minutes

Silence   3 minutes

Shared Readings

I have the audacity to believe that peoples everywhere can have three meals a day for their bodies, education and culture for their minds, and dignity, equality and freedom for their spirits. I believe that what self-centered men have torn down men other-centered can build up.

—Martin Luther King Jr.

You cannot be fair to others without first being fair to yourself.

—Vera Nazarian

Life is not spread evenly for all people, but by reaching out to others we can even it out more. Life is not fair, but by watching out for and supporting one another we can make it more fair.... It is not even or fair or just. That is our work: to bring more fairness and justice and love into life.

—Douglas Taylor

I think the law of life is karma. Actions produce consequences, and these consequences are inescapable. They are not, however, unalterable; they can be altered, for better or for worse, by further action. Every living being runs up a karma-account; ... a karma-account is never closed because the series of rebirths is endless.

—Arnold Toynbee

You reap whatever you sow.

—Galatians 6:7

It can not have failed to strike you that these men ask for just, the same thing—*fairness*, and fairness only. This, so far as in my power, they, and all others, shall have.

—Abraham Lincoln

Live so that when your children think of fairness, caring, and integrity, they think of you.

—H. Jackson Brown Jr.

Sharing   60 minutes

Closing Circle

Extinguishing the Chalice

We extinguish this flame, and we remember the warmth of our community, the light of our wisdom, the generosity of our sharing. We keep these in our heart until we meet again. [Extinguish the chalice.]

Song/Silence

Announcements

SEVEN

Cultivating Ourselves

❧

BEFORE YOU GATHER

One must finally stop, find repose, and send down roots to culti-
vate one's garden.
—John Bryant

To cultivate anything, be it a plant, an animal, a mind, is to make
grow. Growth, expansion is the end. Nothing admits culture, but
that which has a principle of life capable of being expanded. He,
therefore, who does what he can to unfold all his powers and capaci-
ties, especially his nobler ones, so as to become a well-proportioned,
vigorous, excellent, happy being, practises self-culture.
—William Ellery Channing

I also know that we must cultivate our garden.
—Voltaire

Consider This

The idea that part of the human vocation is to cultivate our-
selves and nurture and grow our own character is found in the
oldest of the world's literatures. But it took a particularly Ameri-
can form with the writings of the Transcendentalists, that body

of mostly Unitarian early-to-mid-nineteenth-century thinkers. They included Henry David Thoreau, Ralph Waldo Emerson, and William Ellery Channing. They popularized the idea about cultivating ourselves and expanded it to include not just the educated or upper classes but everybody. By virtue of our humanity, they taught, everyone has a duty develop his or her gifts, expand his or her talents, add to human knowledge, and develop spiritually, and to do so throughout our lives. The Transcendentalists called this sacred duty *self-culture.*

In those days, the word *culture* was not associated with concerts and art galleries but rather with agriculture. *Culture* referred to encouraging or cultivating the growth of plants. The duty of self-culture was first articulated by Rev. William Ellery Channing, an early nineteenth-century Unitarian minister. As a part of his ministry, he was a popular public speaker in Boston. His delivered his lecture "Self-Culture" in 1838 in Boston to an audience of manual laborers. He wanted to enhance the self-concept of these men and women. He went to some pains to proclaim that each and every one of them was a child of God and possessed a soul that made him or her great, no matter the trade they pursued. Channing told these manual laborers that self-culture is the duty we owe ourselves. This is our human calling, he said: to care for ourselves and unfold and perfect ourselves.

Channing spoke and wrote to a wide audience about both personal and ethical growth. They had to do with the quality of our own lives and of our relationships with others and actions toward others. In his Christian milieu, it was not necessary for him to emphasize our duties to others, for that was very well developed in the culture. It was much more countercultural at that time to advocate the idea that we have a duty to cultivate aspects of our inner lives, such as self-respect, self-care, wisdom, and peace of mind. However, the side of self-culture that involves our ability to act ethically, understand, empathize with and care for others, and attempt to influence society for the better was also very important to Channing, who was a social activist and abolitionist.

Channing went so far as to claim that self-culture is our salvation and the most important part of our lives. Through his writings, the phrase *salvation by character*—which meant finding ultimate meaning in life by developing our character—became one of the watchwords of nineteenth-century Unitarianism.

Self-culture is an old-fashioned sounding phrase, but the idea it points to is worthy and important. Personal growth is a critical part of the meaning and satisfaction we find throughout our lives. So is ethical growth, or our willingness to extend ourselves for others, either in the private or public realm. While individuals will naturally find different balances between these two foci, both are critical. The person who only attends to their inner growth and is content to tend their own garden, with no thought of contributing to the human enterprise, is living an impoverished life. As is the person whose only concern is saving the world but who has not developed the wisdom to manage their disappointments with human nature.

A more contemporary term for self-culture might be *cultivating ourselves*. When we engage in this activity, we are in the interesting position of being both the garden *and* the gardener who is doing the cultivation. This ability to use our minds to mold our minds (all while being a mind and having a mind) seems to be the greatest gift of higher consciousness. And using our greatest and most human gifts brings great satisfaction to our lives.

Channing told his audience of laborers that we humans have two powers that make it possible to cultivate the garden of ourselves: self-searching and self-forming. Self-searching is our ability to watch ourselves, notice patterns, and remember our past. Self-forming is the ability to decide to change directions, break habits, form new ones, and take ourselves in hand and try something new. We can figure ourselves out, in other words, guide our own growth, curb our own behavior, control our own passions, and impel our own learning.

We decide, perhaps, that we are going to come out of our naturally introverted shell and make friends in a new community. We notice that we tend to choose solitary tasks and isolate ourselves. We make a plan, therefore, and pick out events to attend, require ourselves to make eye contact with strangers, and speak with the people we meet. We learn how to make small talk and force ourselves to ask others about their lives. As we experiment with these strategies, we celebrate small successes and check the things we have tried off our list of tasks.

Or perhaps we decide we are going to do our own taxes this year, get involved in politics, get out of the debt habit, or slow down and really listen to our spouse or children. We search ourselves for the actions, habits, and patterns that might impede our chosen goal, and we make a plan. We become gardeners of our own souls.

No doubt most people through the ages have believed that we are able to make decisions, break habits, and so on. Channing's particular contribution to human thought was to convincingly state that self-culture is spiritual growth. He believed that the impulse in us to grow and develop is divine and that when we go with its flow—whether we are quitting smoking, caring for others, or requiring ourselves to do what we think is right—we are doing the religious work of cultivating our moral self, and this work is what connects us to the divine.

Channing believed that cultivating oneself requires intellectual skills, for it uses the mind's powers to seek, reason, judge, and learn. Objectivity and the ability to seek truth no matter how uncomfortable are crucial traits of the person dedicated to self-culture. He told those laborers to whom he lectured in 1838 that education is not simply the acquiring of facts but the cultivation of the ability to think. He felt so strongly about education that he finished his lecture by remarking that the foundation of self-culture lies in a basic education in childhood, without which a person is crippled for life. He commended to his audience the "recent exertions of our legislature and private citizens, on behalf of our public schools, the chief hope of our country." He then suggested that some part of the public lands of the nation be consecrated to the education of youth, which indeed they were in the land grant colleges of our nation.

We might imagine that his audience of laborers went home that night lifted in spirit. Perhaps they were newly aware of themselves as worthy beings who, as they worked their jobs, read their newspapers, ruminated over their lives, grieved their losses, cared for their children, and conversed with their buddies, were not simply indulging themselves but cultivating their characters. Channing taught that they were not only living but finding salvation—the wholeness and health and moral growth that point us to what we are meant to be.

Channing's choice to use the language of cultivation for our human capacity of self-directed growth and development is very apt. Gardeners know, for instance, that while they must plan the garden and lay out and perform the tasks of cultivation, the growth that happens is one of those natural phenomena that can only be called a miracle. The gardener helps along a natural process and can look at the harvest—that basket of tomatoes or armful of flowers—as a wonderful collaboration between wisdom, labor, and the great powers of growth and renewal, which no gardener can create and for which gratitude is the only appropriate response. Nor is a gardener in control of the process. The most well-tended plants sometimes just don't do well, and the gardener must continually adjust to nature.

Our self-cultivation is similar. We may set a goal of making a contribution to our world by becoming politically active and choose the school board election as the cause closest to our hearts and seemingly most accessible. But we may find that our attempts to get elected lead to disappointment. Instead of continuing to try to force our initial decision to bear fruit, it might be time for a change in focus. The good gardener learns from the plants that don't thrive but doesn't indulge in self-blame, and neither should the cultivator of self. When it comes to taking new directions in our lives, we can adopt an attitude of experimentation and an awareness that, like the gardener, we're not in control of most of the crucial factors. This will help us to gracefully back off of what's not bearing fruit in our lives and try new directions.

The good gardener works with reverence for nature's gifts, including the gifts that come through the gardener: labor, knowledge, perseverance, and hope. The person who has embarked on cultivating the self will do well to have a similar reverence for both sides of the cultivation equation. Just as the gardener takes credit for her labor and honors nature's miracle of growth, so the self-cultivator gives herself credit for the hard work of growth and the strengths she has previously developed, and she honors the gifts of love and help from those around her and her own natural impulses to grow, learn, and better herself.

A good gardener is also realistic, adapting plans to reality and working with nature. It's nearly impossible to grow blueberries in the soil of the southwest or oranges in northern climes. There are avenues of self-culture that are probably closed to us as well. We have to understand and work with the personality, body, skills, and past that we have and make realistic plans for our self-development. If math has always come hard and numbers are a mystery, it would be foolish to attempt to embark on an engineering career. The person whose childhood has left them with a scarred heart may find that their contribution to the world must be made with animals or as a lone scholar. Finding the right goals and best containers for our personal growth is part of what a good gardener learns to do.

Finally, the good gardener takes a holistic view of the situation in planning the garden. Even if eggplants grow wonderfully in her climate and she herself loves their beautiful color and variety, if nobody around her likes eggplant, she should probably not make the cultivation of eggplant her life work. Gardening, like self-culture, requires balancing the gardener's satisfaction with the needs of the world. Similarly, as we choose our own goals as we cultivate ourselves, it's important to think about what the world needs from us right now, as well as what goals will give us the most satisfaction. In his book *Wishful Thinking*, writer-minister Frederick Buechner put this duty best: "The place God calls you to is the place where your deep gladness and the world's deep hunger meet."

These days community organizers talk about "capacity build-ing" as they help groups of people figure out how to make their communities better. The gardener's work could also be considered as capacity-building. No matter what he plants, he will work the soil to make it more fertile, make wise and careful choices of crops and varieties and planting conditions, be diligent about water-ing and weeding, and even take out plants that are not thriving. A good gardener tends not only the garden but the compost pile, and cares not only about the plants but the soil and the needs of those who will use the product. All this thought and care builds the garden's capacity to produce more food, products, or beauty.

Similarly, we have a duty to ourselves to always build our own capacities: to learn, to keep our hearts open, to discover the ethi-cal way and follow it, to develop our creativity and our ability to care. Whatever specific goals or products we tend, we will notice the whole ecology of our situation and appreciate both the good-ness of nature and the needs of the people around us. When we are about that, we are truly cultivating the garden of our lives.

Activities and Questions

1. What's already in the garden of your life that pleases you (traits, skills, desires, etc.)? What needs to go? What would you like to encourage with extra TLC?

2. Who are some fellow gardeners in your life (books, compan-ions, helpers, etc.)?

3. Channing thought that there were two areas in which we cul-tivate ourselves: our interior lives (including patience, self-discipline, or mindfulness) and our ethical lives (including the courage to stand up for what is right, being courteous to oth-ers, caretaking). Are there traits in both these areas that you would like to cultivate in yourself?

4. How are you a good gardener as you go about cultivating yourself? Are you kind to yourself? Patient? Careful to set realistic goals?

5. Channing spoke of our ability to watch ourselves, notice patterns, and remember our past. He called this self-searching. When have you successfully made a change in yourself using this approach?

6. Channing called the ability to decide to change directions, break habits, or try something new our ability to self-form. When have you done some of these?

7. What do you think of the idea that the work of self-development is guided by us (the gardeners), but the miracle of growth is an awesome natural phenomena? Can you tell a story of self-development that seemed to blossom on its own in your life?

Thinking about the Words of the Day

Before coming to the gathering, think of a few words, phrases, or metaphors that describe self-cultivation. The prompt for the Words of the Day activity will be to complete this sentence: "The areas of myself I'd like to cultivate are . . ."

~

GATHERING

Words of the Day

The areas of myself I'd like to cultivate are . . .

Chalice Lighting

We light this chalice [candle, lamp, etc.] to shine on our time together. In its light we celebrate the relationships and understanding we are creating in this place and time. May our sharing be deep. [Light the chalice.]

The Basket

Responsive Reading

Leader: The words we share . . .

Response: *come from our hearts, our minds, our lives.*

Leader: The feelings we express . . .

Response: *are real, important, and a part of the human heritage we all share.*

Leader: The ties we create in this community . . .

Response: *remind us of the web of creation, of which we are a part.*

On Our Hearts   10 minutes

Silence   3 minutes

Shared Readings

Cultivating the soil can be a powerful spiritual exercise. Working in our gardens takes us on a journey of discovery within and around us, deepening our connection to nature and ourselves.
    —Diane Dreher

Solitude is the soil in which genius is planted, creativity grows, and legends bloom; faith in oneself is the rain that cultivates a hero to endure the storm, and bare the genesis of a new world, a new forest.
    —Mike Norton

The seed is in the ground.
Now may we rest in hope
While darkness does its work.
    —Wendell Berry

The unexamined life is not worth living.
    —Plato

All parts of a tree speak. The roots tell about the dark underground life in the soil—like our own soul life—that sustains growth.
    —Elizabeth Murray

What a gloomy thing, not to know the address of one's soul?
    —Victor Hugo

I want to unfold.
Let no place in me hold itself closed.
    —Rainer Maria Rilke

Soul care resembles a tree. It takes years for a tender tree to mature. Time, attention, nourishment, protection, and pruning contribute to its growth. The same is true for spiritual growth.
    —Stephen W. Smith

Sharing   60 minutes

Closing Circle

Extinguishing the Chalice

We extinguish this flame, and we remember the warmth of our community, the light of our wisdom, the generosity of our sharing. We keep these in our heart until we meet again. [Extinguish the chalice.]

Song/Silence

Announcements

EIGHT

Strangers

∽

BEFORE YOU GATHER

This being human is a guest house.
Every morning a new arrival.

A joy, a depression, a meanness,
Some momentary awareness comes
As an unexpected visitor.

Welcome and entertain them all!
Even if they're a crowd of sorrows,
who violently sweep your house
empty of its furniture,
still treat each guest honorably.
He may be clearing you out
for some new delight.

The dark thought, the shame, the malice,
meet them at the door laughing,
and invite them in.

Be grateful for whoever comes,
because each has been sent
as a guide from beyond.
    —Jalal al-Din Rumi, translated by Coleman Barks

Consider This

Scripture and folk wisdom is full of stories of strangers who give unexpected gifts. The Greeks told the story of Baucis and Philemon, a poor, elderly couple who put out their last porridge for the disguised gods Jupiter and Mercury. They were rewarded with their greatest wish, which was to die together. In the Hebrew scriptures, Abraham and Sara, also an elderly couple, were good to visiting angels and were rewarded with the news that Sara was pregnant with their first child. She was ninety and laughed, but nine months later, the baby was born.

In China, they tell of the Dragon of Wu. When a besieged village prayed for a dragon to save them from marauding bands, nothing seemed to happen, but that evening a small man came into the village leaning on a bamboo staff and asked for hospitality. This was reluctantly given but in the morning, when the gates were once again near breaking, he turned into a magnificent dragon and chased the enemies away.

These stories tell us many things. They tell us about the ethos, if not the history, of times past. They speak of our deep obligation to extend hospitality to the stranger, born not only out of the needs of human community but out of our own need to experience something or someone new. They speak of the gifts that strangers bring. They tell us something about our inner life, about how we help those around us and experience growth. And they speak of the conditions of hospitality, which are not wealth and decorations, fine food or glorious surroundings, but an open heart to the stranger and an open mind to a new idea.

We're programmed to be wary of strangers, some of us more strongly than others, programmed not only by our parents' admonitions and community's fears but by our very genes. No sooner does a baby's maturing brain figure out that she is a separate creature from others than she develops stranger anxiety. One of the first things that happens to a frightened community is that they turn on the strangers among them. Post-9/11 America was not a good place to be—or even seem to be—a stranger.

Perhaps because fear of strangers and the tendency to mistreat strangers is so strong in us, one of the common messages of the world's religions is to do just the opposite—to welcome the stranger, to offer hospitality to the traveler, to think of strangers not as threatening but as interesting, and to consider that opportunity to know them as enriching. This is hard work for most of us. The care of strangers is one of those biblical values that makes some people feel nervous rather than warm and fuzzy.

Most of us are not confronted by wayfarers at our doors, but many of us regularly confront strangers asking us for money on the streets or people who don't look or act or sound like us and who require extra energy to understand or even be kind to. This cost is both the price and the blessing of community, and in our ever-larger and more diverse communities, we confront strangers ever more often. It's a strain, but also a blessing. When diversity comes with a human face, we are more likely to be able to open our minds and hearts to all that is new to us. It's an important spiritual and intellectual discipline.

One of the interesting things about congregations, especially the larger ones, is that they are one of the few places for most people where we regularly, and happily, greet, shake hands with, and smile at perfect strangers. Why does this feel good? Perhaps because it is so unique in our lives. It feels good to be reassured that the world's strangers are really okay.

A community disaster brings out something of that same benefit. The needs of the moment mean that strangers work together and help each other and it feels good to see this in action—even from our TV sets. It makes us feel uplifted.

But these are fleeting moments in our lives unless we take the trouble to practice what is really a spiritual discipline as well as the advice of the world's faiths: to be kind to strangers, curious rather than condemning, and therefore able to receive their gifts.

Taken metaphorically, stories about hospitality to strangers refer not just to people we don't know but to all new things in our lives. The stranger you are most in need of greeting in your life could be a new idea, a dream, a risk. Perhaps the stranger at your door is a transgender bathroom down the hall or that nagging feeling that you need to re-think what you have always believed about God or immigration or tax policy or your retirement.

The stranger in your life could be a grief, a depression, an unwelcome development. Will you slam the door? Can you be curious? Is there anything to learn?

Keeping our hearts and minds open to the new is one of the two basics of religious liberalism. Conservative religion looks to truth in old books, established wisdom, time-honored doctrines. Religious liberals find those things interesting and often instructive but tend to treat them as a starting place for our thinking, adding human wisdom and our own intuition to the mix. Then there is the strangest stranger of all, the one inside of us who we don't know. The one whose anger surprises us, whose strength saves us, whose slips embarrass us, whose misdeeds can bring us down. That's a stranger worth knowing—and when we do, we're less likely to be hijacked by their frantic bids for attention.

According to Carl Jung, the stranger inside, whom he called our shadow, is born of necessity, when we need or choose a trait or talent as a focus for our personality and repress the mirror trait. A child who is not permitted to express anger may have an unconscious angry streak. A person who has decided to develop their musical ability may have a disappointed mathematician as a shadow. These traits tend to pop out when we are not paying attention, causing so-called Freudian slips. Sometimes we say, "I just don't know what got into me . . ." Actually nothing got into you, rather, something got out of you, one of your strangers within.

While it is delightful to discover an inner artist who was discouraged in grade school, most of the strangers inside us are a little more challenging. The sullen child who didn't get what she needed, the angry adolescent, or the resentful spouse can be difficult and embarrassing. However, the more we know them, the less trouble they are likely to cause us.

We get to know those strangers within through self-reflection, by asking ourselves why we feel the way we do, why we keep making the same mistakes, where our strengths and weaknesses come from. We get to know the stranger inside through meditation, therapy, dream work, and other adventures in self-knowledge. We get to know the stranger inside when we ask ourselves what it is about the strangers and strange ideas in our lives that bothers us so much. Indeed, some of the greatest gifts strangers can give us are these rare clues to unknown parts of ourselves. And the habit of being kind to strangers and open-minded to new ideas can help us take a fearless and kind look at the parts of ourselves that we'd rather not see but which are often important parts of our lives.

We offer hospitality to the stranger inside mostly by compassionate recognition. If our childhood has left us with an inner class clown, or a traumatic experience has given us an inner hurt child, mostly all this character wants is recognition and perhaps a little protection, or a chance to get out and play in a safe way.

Whether the stranger at our door is a challenging person, a new-fangled idea, or the inner class clown who just made a fool of us, both folk wisdom and religious wisdom have similar recommendations for dealing with strangers. First of all, we have to let the stranger in the door. That means firmly setting aside our natural tendency to turn our backs on difference and bringing forward our kind self for a new person, our open-minded self for a new idea, and our compassionate self for the stranger inside.

Secondly, we need to suspend judgment long enough to learn a little more about the stranger, to wonder about what has confronted us, and to muster our curiosity about what the good points of this experience might be.

Thirdly, we need to keep a reserve of energy in our lives so that we are able to cope with the inevitable strangers who are going to come through and disrupt things. It is so hard to remember to be hospitable when we're in the thick of our challenges and miseries, when we have just enough in our lives and not really quite enough more for the unwelcome visitor. And there is little in our cultural wisdom right now to remind us to make room. We have to remember the old stories, the foreign poems, and the ancient scriptures that advise us to invite strangers in, offer them food—even if it means sharing our crumbs—and let them stay a bit.

To give hospitality, the stories say, we must be poor. Not necessarily poor in material things but living with enough space in our lives, minds, and hearts for others. If I am utterly "full of myself," distracted by my own worries, tensions, and issues, or even distracted by my decorations and fancy cooking, I cannot attend to others. When I am restless, have too much to do, am too driven by thousands of different stimuli, well, my life is already full, and there is not room in my psychic home for a guest, and even the most welcome cannot enter without feeling a bit like an intruder.

On a physical level we understand this; when we are planning a party we clear out the hall closet so that there will be room for the guests' coats. At church, we put out more chairs than we expect to need so that the visitors will have a choice of seats and latecomers will feel welcome. We even build whole new buildings so that all who want to come in can be welcomed! These are all issues of making space so that we can be hospitable. The same thing is true of making psychic space. If we are consumed with our own needs, in a rush to get everything done, we will not have psychic space to share with others, to entertain new ideas, to ponder the new feelings welling up in us.

Our lives are often so full that there is no room for others, sometimes not even room for ourselves. If our lives are planned and orchestrated too completely, there is no space for the unexpected, the strange, the wonderful. Have faith! Leave some space for a stranger.

Activities and Questions

1. Think about the strangers in your life recently. List a few of them. Try to think of one in each of the four categories:

- a stranger you have experienced in your daily work or life in the past few weeks
- a stranger in the form of an idea, dream, or risk that is starting to make you feel uncomfortable
- a stranger from within who pops out in embarrassing over-reactions or slips of the tongue
- an unwelcome visitor who comes into your life, like grief, depression, or an unwelcome development

2. Think of a time when you were able to be hospitable to a different kind of person, a new idea, or a newly discovered part of yourself.
3. Describe a time when you had to befriend an unwelcome development in your life and later discovered that you learned something important.
4. Think of an idea you hold that is starting to make you feel uneasy. Maybe it's something in a sermon that makes you squirm or the hint of a prejudice you have that you aren't ready to change but that you keep noticing like a thorn that keeps pricking you.
5. How do you practice hospitality to strangers, new ideas, parts of yourself?
6. Tell about a time when you experienced the joy of solidarity with lots of different kinds of people, such as working together after a disaster.
7. To get a sense of an inner stranger, try this. Name three or four people you don't like and list the reasons you don't like them. Later, cross out the names of the people and insert your own name. Re-read the list and consider whether you may have stumbled on parts of your inner stranger.

Thinking about the Words of the Day

Before coming to the gathering, think of a few words, phrases, or metaphors that describe some of the strangers—human, experiential, or inner—that you have become aware of in your lives. The prompt for the Words of the Day activity will be to complete this sentence: "Strangers in my life recently are . . ."

∾

GATHERING

Words of the Day

Strangers in my life recently are . . .

Chalice Lighting

We light this chalice [candle, lamp, etc.] to shine on our time together. In its light we celebrate the relationships and understanding we are creating in this place and time. May our sharing be deep. [Light the chalice.]

The Basket

Responsive Reading

Leader: The words we share . . .

Response: *come from our hearts, our minds, our lives.*

Leader: The feelings we express . . .

Response: *are real, important, and a part of the human heritage we all share.*

Leader: The ties we create in this community . . .

Response: *remind us of the web of creation, of which we are a part.*

On Our Hearts   10 minutes

Silence   3 minutes

Shared Readings

We must also remember
That at every meeting we are meeting a stranger.
—T. S. Eliot

Sometimes . . . we need to be strangers to ourselves. Then the hidden light in our souls will illuminate what we need to see.
—Paulo Coelho

Let mutual love continue. Do not neglect to show hospitality to strangers, for by doing that some have entertained angels without knowing it.
—Hebrews 13:1–2

Make yourself a door through which
to be hospitable, even to the stranger in you.
—David Whyte

In the Buddhist tradition, our connections are real; our separations are an illusion. . . . If you and I are ultimately connected, you cannot be other. You cannot be an alien, a foreigner. If I do not know you I do not yet know a part of my self. When you and I are separated, neither of us is whole.
—Peter Morales

We meet no Stranger but Ourself.
—Emily Dickinson

God speaks, and God is to be heard, not only on Sinai, not only in my own heart, but in the voice of *the stranger.*
—Thomas Merton

In each one of us there is another whom we do not know. He speaks to us in dreams and tells us how differently he sees us from the way we see ourselves. When, therefore, we find ourselves in a difficult situation, to which there is no solution, he can sometimes kindle a light that radically alters our attitude—the very attitude that led us into the difficult situation.

—Carl Jung

Sharing 60 minutes

Closing Circle

Extinguishing the Chalice

We extinguish this flame, and we remember the warmth of our community, the light of our wisdom, the generosity of our sharing. We keep these in our heart until we meet again. [Extinguish the chalice.]

Song/Silence

Announcements

NINE

Mental Wellness

∾

BEFORE YOU GATHER

But I'm not crazy, I'm just a little unwell
I know right now you can't tell
But stay awhile and maybe then you'll see
A different side of me
   —Rob Thomas

At one time or another, most people go through a period of sadness, trial, loss, frustration, or failure that is so disturbing and long-lasting that it can be called a dark night of the soul.
   —Thomas Moore

For me stigma means fear, resulting in lack of confidence. Stigma is loss, resulting in unresolved mourning issues. Stigma is not having access to resources, resulting in lack of useful coping skills. Stigma is being invisible or being reviled, resulting in conflicts regarding being seen. Stigma is lowered family esteem and intense shame, resulting in decreased self-worth. Stigma is secrecy, resulting in lack of understanding. Stigma is judgment, resulting in lack of spontaneity. Stigma is divisive, resulting in distrust of others. Stigma is anger, resulting in distance. Most importantly, stigma is hopelessness, resulting in helplessness. This all adds up to decreased potential, of self and for others.

—Mary Gullekson

It is recognised that mental health and illness are part of a continuum. . . . There is no universal definition of what is normal or abnormal and in this context what constitutes mental health or mental illness. . . . Depending on a variety of circumstances, individuals move along the continuum from health to illness and may stop at key points for varying lengths of time.

—Mary Chambers

Consider This

I (Christine Robinson) did part of my training for ministry as a chaplain in a federal mental hospital in Washington, D.C. This was just at the end of the era when people were regularly confined to a mental institution for life. On my first ward of elderly patients there were still some long-term residents who didn't want to leave the only home they had known for years. It was a very stressful first assignment. Many of those for whom I was supposed to be providing pastoral care didn't talk and almost all came from the South and the Black church, a culture and a religious tradition that I didn't know much about. Nor did I yet know much about mental illness or aging. I am naturally shy, and I was twenty-six years old. I wanted to help but I had no earthly idea what to do when the ward door locked behind me each morning.

The first week was bewildering. Patients mostly wanted cigarettes and lights from me. This was a long time ago and the whole social structure of the place revolved around smoking. At first I tried to get around this; it seemed immoral to support what I knew to be a dangerous habit. So it was with some alarm that I noticed, as the days passed, an increasingly strong desire to have a smoke myself, something I had never felt before. I was shocked at myself. I had not realized I could even entertain such a foolish idea. But no amount of rational self-talk worked. I was becoming obsessed with the desire to smoke.

And then the weather turned miserably hot and containers of ice water with ladles and cups appeared on the hot wards. Suddenly, the social dynamic started revolving around ice water as well as smoking. Around that time, one of the patients I hadn't interacted with appeared at my side, looked at my misery and frustration and discomfort with compassion, and said, "Chaplain, honey, may I get you a cup of ice water?"

She did and we sat down together, and she told me about her life. She had been a patient on what was now a geriatric ward since she was a teenager, following a mental breakdown caused by a rape. She had her good days and her bad days. This was a good enough day that she noticed a clumsy and suffering chaplain and did what she could to help. On that day I started my work as a chaplain. And on that day, my desire to smoke wafted away and never returned.

I learned a lot that summer. First and foremost, I learned that a diagnosis and a history and a label are all only parts of the totality of a person's humanity, and that each of us—whether healthy, ill, or disabled—has a way to serve, a life to live, a light to shine. I also learned that mental health is not something that some people have and others, "the mentally ill," don't have. Like physical health, mental health is a continuum with a bell-curve. There are a few people so sturdy and blessed that they enjoy shining mental health through their entire lives. There are a few others who are so debilitated by poor mental health that they need considerable support to function at all. Most of us are in between, and most of us experience better and worse mental health during different times in our lives—times when we can be more or less easily captured by our moods, our addictions, our worries, or the traumas of our past. The Centers for Disease Control (CDC) estimates that 50 percent of Americans will, at some point in our lives, seek help for our distress and get a diagnosis, and almost all of us who do will eventually work ourselves into a healthier place again.

As I learned about the people I was supposed to be caring for that summer, I learned about myself. I realized that, even in my twenty-six years, I had already suffered various bouts of mental unwellness. There was a summer of grief at losing a beloved chorus teacher. There was an entire college semester of what I now understood was a classic depression: waking in tears in the small hours of the night, feeling inept at all I did, a depression that cleared up on its own after about three months, as often happens. There was "stage fright" so great that I was unable to demonstrate what I knew I could do, which I now understand as an anxiety that had been disabling to my dreams. I had never thought of those things as akin to mental illness, had never sought help, had never allowed myself to think that I might have anything in common with someone suffering from mental illness. It was an enlightening summer!

Later in the summer, I served as the chaplain on an admission ward, where people came for a few days to get their medication regulated, begin a care plan, or otherwise get back to functioning safely. With these patients, I realized that medications can have the same miraculous effect on mental illness as they do on physical illness and that a healing environment can do the same. We humans are body and mind, inexorably twined together.

The CDC tells us that of the nearly half of Americans who will be diagnosed with a mental condition at some point during their lifetimes, about 6 percent will have a serious mental illness and will be extremely disabled for some time. This means that the prevalence of mental illness is about the same as the prevalence of cancer and heart disease. Most sufferers of cancer and heart disease recover. Likewise, most sufferers of mental illness recover. Treatment, time, and lifestyle changes do their work and the patients return to the ranks of the healthy, sometimes with lingering impairments, usually with new pills to take, and often worried about a recurrence.

Like cancer and heart disease, mental illness causes a lot of suffering, does a lot of economic damage, and sometimes kills. Ninety percent of persons who commit suicide have a diagnosable mental illness, and often people who are struggling with mental illness don't take good care of themselves, which can lead to physical health complications. And while some heart or cancer patients feel they have to deal with some stigma about their illness, virtually all mental health patients feel the weight of society's prejudices, ignorance, and denial of mental illness. Stigma is a negative prejudice that falls on people in a certain group, defining them as inferior, irresponsible, dangerous, scary, losers, and so on, just because of one characteristic. It's a big burden, an awful load to dump on someone who is already dealing with a health issue.

You may have been surprised at the prevalence of mental health conditions and illness in the population. One problem with stigma is that people who are in the stigmatized group don't talk about it. Naturally enough, they want to sidestep the burden of dealing with others' prejudices. This deprives them of support and those around them of opportunities to realize that their information is incorrect and their prejudices harmful. Stigma makes it harder for people to ask for or accept treatment and makes it easier for the government or taxpayers or insurance companies to deny treatment.

One way we all can lessen the stigma of mental illness is to watch our language, for our language influences how we think and it telegraphs that to others. For instance, the term *the mentally ill* suggests that everyone diagnosed with a mental condition is alike enough and debilitated enough that they can be lumped in one, all-defining category, as if nothing else in their lives mattered. We don't talk about "the cancerous" or "the heart diseased" as categories of human beings. We give those sufferers the dignity of *having* an illness as one part of themselves, rather than *being* an illness and nothing else. We're aware that some kinds of cancer are a nuisance, some require strenuous treatment, and some are fatal. Mental illness is the same way. That goes for specific diagnoses, too. Saying that someone *is* schizophrenic or *is* bipolar is saying something like "that's the definition of you" and implies "and I don't care about anything else." People have schizophrenia like they have cancer. It's a part of their lives—it may be a huge part of their lives—but it's not them.

Another interesting glitch in our language is that technical terms for mental illness become popularly used to mean dysfunctional or off-beat thinking in general. Once these terms become informal, they are used as slang for the mentally ill. For instance, once it was thought that the phases of the moon affected the severely mentally ill, who were called "lunatics" and often cared for in "lunatic asylums." Now we say things like "that would be lunacy," meaning "that would be a very bad idea!" And we informally refer to the severely mentally ill as "looney" and mental hospitals as "loony bins." Lately a new bit of slang has appeared among the young: "Are you mental?" This doesn't mean "Are you mentally ill?" It means the same thing as the questions of previous generations: "Are you crazy?" "Are you nuts?" "Are you cracked?" "Are you mad?" "Are you insane?" Some of this language is hurtful to those who suffer mental illness, so we should be careful. It is always best to avoid using global labels for persons ("Are you mental?") and instead be more precise about what we're communicating ("I don't think that would be a good idea").

A courageous way to combat stigma is to take the radical and countercultural step of treating our own mental health challenges like we treat our physical health challenges. If we just come out and talk about it, brave prejudice when it happens, seek treatment when we need it, and let mental health be just a regular part of health, things will be a lot easier. Normalizing mental illness and treatment and the lifestyle and medication adjustments that keep us well will only happen if ordinary people start talking about their whole lives.

Maybe you are one of those shiningly healthy persons who has no mental health worries at all and never remembers having any. But . . . probably not. Most of us have had seasons of depression, days or weeks when our anxiety, with or without obvious cause, affected our work and our relationships. Some of us have had moments, hours, or even weeks where we were delusional, and we recovered and moved on with our lives. Some of us always have to husband our mental health and watch our stress levels, take medication, get out in the sun, and exercise, just as some of us have to watch our physical health (often in exactly the same ways!).

In order to live openhearted and openminded lives, it is good for us to be aware of mental health issues and how they affect us and our friends and loved ones. It is also good to take the risk of breaking the taboo about sharing our stories around mental wellness and unwellness.

Activities and Questions

1. Think back to a time when you felt unwell. This might be postpartum depression, feeling overwhelmed and lonely in college, experiencing grief after a marriage breakup, spending a year in denial, or struggling with an addiction. How did you feel? What symptoms did you notice? What helped and what didn't as you moved through this time?

2. Perhaps you cope regularly with the mental illness of a family member or friend. If the latter, as you share in the group, remember to talk mostly about yourself, giving only those details about the other person that are necessary to explain your own experience, thoughts, and feelings. How has knowing a person with mental health challenges changed you?

3. Does the often stigmatizing language surrounding mental health trouble you? What are you able to do about that?

4. Listen to the song "Unwell" by the band Matchbox 20. It can be found on YouTube and iTunes.

Thinking about the Words of the Day

Before coming to the gathering, think of a few words, phrases, or metaphors that describe a time of your own unwellness. The prompt for the Words of the Day activity will be to complete this sentence: "My time of unwellness was/was like . . ."

~

GATHERING

Words of the Day

My time of unwellness was/was like . . .

Chalice Lighting

We light this chalice [candle, lamp, etc.] to shine on our time together. In its light we celebrate the relationships and understanding we are creating in this place and time. May our sharing be deep. [Light the chalice.]

The Basket

Responsive Reading

Leader: The words we share . . .

Response: *come from our hearts, our minds, our lives.*

Leader: The feelings we express . . .

Response: *are real, important, and a part of the human heritage we all share.*

Leader: The ties we create in this community . . .

Response: *remind us of the web of creation, of which we are a part.*

On Our Hearts   10 minutes

Silence   3 minutes

Shared Readings

In the next year or two or three, you or someone you love will sink into a depression. That dark abyss can lead to a living death and to death itself. But we need not be afraid of the dark. We must not deny depression in ourselves or in others. We must help each other face and overcome depression. Now, more than ever, there is hope.
　　—Peter Morales

Midway along the journey of our life
　　I woke to find myself in some dark woods,
　　for I had wandered off from the straight path.

How hard it is to tell what it was like,
　　this wood of wilderness, savage and stubborn
　　(the thought of it brings back all my old fears)
　　—Dante

I have myself an inner weight of woe
That God himself can scarcely bear.
　　—Theodore Roethke

The hardest thing to practice is not allowing yourself to be overwhelmed by despair.
　　—Thich Nhat Hanh

Real listening always brings people closer together.
Trust that meaningful conversations can change your world.
Rely on human goodness. Stay together.
　　—Meg Wheatley

We need one another when we mourn and would be comforted. We need one another when we are in trouble and afraid. We need one another when we are in despair, in temptation, and need to be recalled to our best selves again. . . . All our lives we are in need, and others are in need of us.

—George E. Odell

Sharing   60 minutes

Closing Circle

Extinguishing the Chalice

We extinguish this flame, and we remember the warmth of our community, the light of our wisdom, the generosity of our sharing. We keep these in our heart until we meet again. [Extinguish the chalice.]

Song/Silence

Announcements

TEN

Miracles

~

BEFORE YOU GATHER

Seeing, hearing, feeling, are miracles, and each part and tag of me
is a miracle.
Divine am I inside and out, and I make holy whatever I touch or
am touched from.
—Walt Whitman

Wine from water is not so small
But an even better magic trick
Is that anything is here at all
So the challenging thing becomes
Not to look for miracles
But finding where there isn't one.
—Peter Mayer

Consider This

There's a story about Jesus that is told no fewer than six times in
the four Gospels—the story of the loaves and the fishes. Although
each version is a little different, the basics are the same. Many peo-
ple have followed Jesus out into the countryside, a long way from
any town, to hear him teach. At the end of the day, the worried

disciples advise Jesus that he needs to quit teaching so that all these people can go and buy food from neighboring farms and villages, but Jesus responds that they should feed the people themselves, presumably out of their own lunch. Because all they have is a few loaves of bread and a few smoked fish, not nearly enough for the multitudes, and possibly also because they want their lunch, they protest that this will be useless because there is not nearly enough to go around. Jesus, no doubt heaving a big sigh, tells them to get the crowd to sit down in groups and to bring him the loaves and fish. He takes their food, blesses it as any good Jewish host would do, and puts it in baskets for the disciples to distribute. They start to do this. Some time passes—if it were a movie, the sound would get hushed and the picture would get fuzzy and a little slow, and there might be a little reverb, and then it would return to real time—and, lo and behold, the whole crowd is eating. All six versions of this story say that everybody eats and is satisfied. The story goes further to say that the baskets are passed again to pick up leftovers, also a Jewish custom, and more food comes back than had originally been served.

Some see this as a contrived miracle story, placed in the Gospels not because anybody remembered anything like that happening but because the authors wanted to give deep roots to the Eucharist ritual, which was well developed in Christian congregations by the time the Gospels were set to paper. Most Christians over the centuries have seen this as a simple miracle story. Jesus had compassion on hungry people, and he used his supernatural powers to create bread for them all—a miracle—which makes many modern people more than a little uncomfortable. But maybe this story did happen and was a miracle of a different sort.

So you are Abraham or Rebecca, a curious sort of person, and you have followed this interesting teacher out into the desert to hear what he has to say, and what he has to say is electrifying. You had to bring your kids, of course, and you knew it was a long way. As a matter of fact, you did come prepared for a long day, because you're no dummy. You have a skin of water and some bread and dried fish and even a few dates stowed away. Enough for your family, but not much more. You have been too excited to eat much, though the kids have had a share, when, toward the end of the afternoon, there is a commotion at the front, near Jesus and his friends. You gather that you are to be seated in small groups with a few others.

Now, all day you have been hearing about love and community and new life but this is the first time you've noticed those around you. As you look around your group, you see a man who is clearly ill, a woman who came with her teenaged daughter, other families, some elders, and a few young men. You gather in a circle and sit. Stretching your neck, you see Jesus blessing a couple of baskets of bread and you see the disciples starting to pass them around. Your group is in the back and nobody is coming your way. All day long you have been hearing about love and community and new life, so what do you do? You smile at the people around you and unwrap the food you have brought, and they do the same. Not everyone has brought food but the love you have heard about and the community you are now sharing with strangers makes what there is go a long way. It is a deeply satisfying meal. Everyone is content, and there are even leftovers to put in the baskets when they go around. Why not? Jesus has to eat, too! The day is lovely, the company is good, all is well.

This is an interpretation of the story that is firmly in the humanistic tradition. Not only does nothing take place to which scientists would object, but it shows human beings at their best: Their hearts are touched by wisdom and they are willing, even happy, to share with each other.

One reason to agree with this interpretation is that not once in those six versions does the Bible say anything like, "And Jesus performed a miracle and suddenly there were enough loaves for everybody." All he does is bless and break the bread, the ordinary actions of a host in that society, and have it passed around. And there is enough for everybody. There's not a hint that he does anything special, intervenes in any laws of physics, or expends any real energy, as happens in others stories when water turns into wine, sick people are healed, or the dead are brought back to life. The miracle, in other words, is in the human hearts of the people who were brought together to share what they had.

Also bolstering this interpretation is that Jesus asks the people to sit face-to-face in small groups. Isn't it true that it is much easier to be generous when there are a few people around us and we look at each other's faces and perhaps even talk about what we have heard? While it is possible to imagine people hoarding their food as they all stand around Jesus, it is harder to imagine that they continue to do so when they are seated, looking at each other. The last detail that seems to authenticate this "miracle" is that Jesus gives his disciples the opportunity to model the sharing, making sharing what we have just a part of how things work around here. No sermon necessary. The miracle is natural, but no less wondrous.

Between this completely naturalistic and heartwarming explanation of how everyone ate that day and the unthinking acceptance of supernatural miracles, there are many ways to think about miracles.

Some who believe that our universe has both a spiritual and natural reality think about miracles this way. Consider a perfectly balanced fish tank, the kind with just enough fish to produce carbon dioxide for the plants and just enough plants to produce food and oxygen for the fish and just enough snails to keep the tank clean. A perfectly functioning system, as nature is. It all works by rules and those rules are natural law in the fish tank. But we, who see the whole picture, know that the fish tank is held by another reality that is outside of it—the reality of the fish tank owner. And while that owner is proud of his perfectly balanced fish tank, a day might come when, say, a new fish, a different kind of plant, and a new breed of snail are introduced. For the fish in the tank, this is a miracle, an intervention in their world that is beyond their understanding. You can't say this breaks the laws of nature and fish tanks. These new elements are subject to the same relentless laws and balances that are the tank's natural system, and they may or may not thrive in that tank. But they got into the system by an intervention from the outside.

Some believe that the natural and spiritual worlds interact, but only through the medium of consciousness. That is to say, God has only our hands and hearts to make the world a better place, and works mightily to persuade me and you to take action to help someone else, and may put other helpful ideas in our minds if we will but take the time to listen. In this worldview, the miracle of the loaves and fishes happened not by multiplication of fishes but by softening of hearts, and that softening was not simply the natural result of human goodness, as the humanists would have it, but by the exertion of spiritual forces on the opened hearts of the crowd. Some people like this explanation because it is both spiritual and congruent with the laws of physics.

Other people find no reason to believe in a spiritual reality at all, but find this natural world and its conscious, loving inhabitants quite miraculous enough. Walt Whitman was one of those. In *Leaves of Grass*, he writes,

> Why! who makes much of a miracle?
> As to me, I know of nothing else but miracles. . . .
>
> To me, every hour of the light and dark is a miracle,
> Every inch of space is a miracle,
> Every square yard of the surface of the earth is spread with the
> same,
> Every cubic foot of the interior swarms with the same;
> Every spear of grass—the frames, limbs, organs, of men and
> women, and all that concerns them,
> All these to me are unspeakably perfect miracles.

Albert Einstein felt the same way. "There are two ways to live your life," he is credited as saying. "One is as if nothing is a miracle. The other is as if everything is a miracle."

Another way to look at miracles is to think of them not as the supernatural breaking into the natural world but as the natural world breaking into the supernatural world. It might go something like this: On one of those terrible days when everything seems out of kilter and going wrong, when everything seems bleak and potentially disastrous and anyway it's stormy and awful, you look up and see a rainbow stretched across the sky. It stops you in your tracks and once you notice it, you also notice that you've come back to yourself, quieter, stronger, and ready to systematically deal with it all.

There is nothing miraculous about a rainbow. Science tells us exactly how one is created and when and why. A rainbow seems to be, as Sylvia Plath says in her poem "The Colossus," one of those "spasmodic tricks of radiance" that are utterly natural but have a nearly universal capacity to touch our hearts and could, therefore, be called a miracle. In this view, what makes something a miracle is that it brings us closer to the whole, deep, spiritual reality of our lives. The rainbow wasn't a miracle, but you looked at it, were comforted and settled in heart, and then went home to treat your children gently. That's when it became a miracle.

The story of the loaves and fishes, however one wants to explain it, can make us extra sensitive to other stories about sharing. So when there is some kind of a disaster and people line up to donate blood or give money or collect household goods, the story of the loaves and fishes might come to mind, reminding us that the impulse to share is one of humanity's sacred stories.

Activities and Questions

1. Name some miracles you have experienced (an opening of the heart, an awe-inspiring moment in nature, loving hands, a birth, healing moments, etc.). What is the meaning of these moments in your life? What have you learned from them?

2. How do you view miracles? Think about possible interactions of the spiritual world and the natural world, as described in the essay.

3. Families sometimes tell stories of miracles through the generations. If your family has such a story, describe it. What does this story mean to you?

4. Look at some of the miracles described in the Bible (healing of the blind, water turned to wine, etc.). What meaning do they have for you?

5. Listen to the song "Holy Now" by Peter Mayer. It is available on YouTube.

Thinking about the Words of the Day

Before coming to the gathering, think of a few words, phrases, or metaphors that describe a miracle. The prompt for the Words of the Day activity will be to complete this sentence: "A miracle is/is like . . ."

GATHERING

Words of the Day

A miracle is/is like . . .

Chalice Lighting

We light this chalice [candle, lamp, etc.] to shine on our time together. In its light we celebrate the relationships and understanding we are creating in this place and time. May our sharing be deep. [Light the chalice.]

The Basket

Responsive Reading

Leader: The words we share . . .

Response: *come from our hearts, our minds, our lives.*

Leader: The feelings we express . . .

Response: *are real, important, and a part of the human heritage we all share.*

Leader: The ties we create in this community . . .

Response: *remind us of the web of creation, of which we are a part.*

On Our Hearts   10 minutes

Silence   3 minutes

Shared Readings

To be a miracle worker you do not have to get a doctoral degree, become a minister, eat a particular food, or be able to meditate for long hours. All you need to do is to begin to see beauty in your life and in those around you.

 —Alan Cohen

"Miracles have ceased." Have they indeed? When? They had not ceased this afternoon when I walked into the wood & got into bright miraculous sunshine in shelter from the roaring wind.

 —Ralph Waldo Emerson

I read these miracle stories as parables with lessons about life and hope and love abundant.

 —Douglas Taylor

People usually consider walking on water or in thin air a miracle. But I think the real miracle is not to walk either on water or in thin air, but to walk on earth. Every day we are engaged in a miracle which we don't even recognize: a blue sky, white clouds, green leaves, the black, curious eyes of a child—our own two eyes. All is a miracle.

 —Thich Nhat Hanh

Miracles occur naturally as expressions of love. The real miracle is the love that inspires them. In this sense everything that comes from love is a miracle.

 —Helen Schucman and William Thetford

Now you will daily give and give, and the great stores of your love will not lessen thereby; for this is the miracle that happens every time to those who really love.

 —Rainer Maria Rilke

Isn't the real miracle creation itself? Isn't the real miracle the fact that there's an order to the universe, natural laws that are discoverable, and unconditional love to be shared in the human realm?
—Scotty McLennan

Sharing   60 minutes

Closing Circle

Extinguishing the Chalice

We extinguish this flame, and we remember the warmth of our community, the light of our wisdom, the generosity of our sharing. We keep these in our heart until we meet again. [Extinguish the chalice.]

Song/Silence

Announcements

ELEVEN

Happiness

❧

BEFORE YOU GATHER

Happiness is as a butterfly which, when pursued, is always beyond our grasp, but which if you will sit quietly, may alight upon you.
— Anonymous, attributed to Nathaniel Hawthorne

If we are not happy and joyous at this season, for what other season shall we wait and for what other time shall we look?
— Abdul-Baha

Every morning, when we wake up, we have twenty-four brand-new hours to live. What a precious gift! We have the capacity to live in a way that these twenty-four hours will bring peace, joy, and happiness to ourselves and others.
— Thich Nhat Hanh

The practice of learning to be happy and aware in the present moment is what the Buddha called "mindfulness" (*smrti*). It's a stable kind of happiness, a happiness we can rely on, because it contains calmness and contentment.
— Thomas Bien

Consider This

Are you happy? Do you feel happy right this minute? How about overall? Being happy is often one of our main goals in life, and we lament it when it seems to go away. By *happiness* we seem to mean a combination of good mood (more positive feelings than negative ones) and a sense of meaning and purpose in life, which comes from being engaged in relationships and work. It is as if these two things are strands of a rope which, twined together, give our lives the flavor of happiness.

We often think that we would be happier if we had more money, better health, better relationships, or more opportunities, but this is not as true as we tend to think it is, in part because these important factors can't easily be teased apart in our lives. For instance, while there is a bewildering variety of research on the subject of what part money plays in human happiness and why, it seems clear that there is no direct association between the two. There is no amount of money or economic attainment in society that will guarantee happiness.

Unhappiness is just as hard to predict. We can easily imagine that we would be very unhappy if our health or relationships took a turn for the worse, and that would probably be true for a while, but most people adjust and come to a new normal and return to about the same level of happiness they enjoyed before things changed for them.

Which brings us back to the twined rope of mood and meaning.

Our life's meaning comes from a sense of contributing to a whole greater than ourselves. This could be family, human knowledge, beauty, the human community, or even a spiritual entity. It is important for our happiness that we have some awareness of what makes life meaningful for us, given what we believe and care about.

It is hard to be happy if we do not have satisfying relationships, so happy people know what kinds of relationships they need to make them happy and cultivate those relationships. Similarly, it is important that at least some of the work of our lives is meaningful to us. This may not be our paid work. Many happy people work for a salary to pay the bills but find the great meaning of their lives in child-rearing, volunteer work, creative or useful hobbies, or social activism. Even in the most limiting of circumstances, such as a nursing home, some people who can do very little in their lives get meaning out of making the day pleasant for the people around them. And most people who get great meaning from their paid work are also engaged in hobbies or family life that makes them happy. It is best if all our eggs of meaning are not in the same basket!

Our mood is also a key aspect of our happiness. Whatever is going on in our lives is colored by our mood—our outlook on life—which is partially genetically determined, a matter of brain chemicals, and so only partly within our control. At the lowest end of the mood scale is depression, an illness that combines low mood, anxiety, sleep and appetite disturbances, and recurring negative thoughts. Depression sometimes starts with a loss or a setback, but sometimes it strikes even when things are going pretty well in life or even after a goal has been reached. Sometimes our brain's chemistry just goes awry. Depression is very uncomfortable and can be dangerous. It is one of the most common causes of lost work days and is one of the major causes of death in our nation. Many people who commit suicide have more accurately died of complications of the disease of depression, which is also a major cause of accidents and the ill health that comes from not taking care of oneself.

Depression can be treated with talk therapy and medications (often both), and is very common in our stressful society. If your mood stays low too long or your thoughts edge into dangerous territory, you might be depressed. If so, your road to happiness should begin with a trip to a physician or therapist. You can search the Internet for the phrase "depression quiz" to check on this yourself in more detail. You can find good ones at governmental or major medical center websites.

Low mood is not simply negative emotions. After all, negative emotions play an important part in our lives. They warn us when things are awry. Animals without emotions like fear, anxiety, or rage tend not to survive in this chancy world. But those emotions tend to narrow our focus to what's wrong right now. That's important in a crisis but limiting in a more complex landscape. Low mood is negative emotions that linger or are not appropriate to the whole of our lives.

Behavioral geneticist David Lykken studied identical twins raised apart and identical twins raised together who were, at the time of the study, experiencing very different circumstances, such as one in a happy marriage and one not. He discovered that identical twins share a very similar happiness level whether or not they were raised together or raised apart, which suggests that our mood is to a great extent, a matter of genetics. To a certain degree, some people are born with a sunny disposition while others with a lower mood. Lykken says that this genetic factor accounts for about half of our mood level; the other half is in our hands. And the combination of good mood and a meaningful life—more than half of which is in our hands!—makes for happiness.

Being happy is important, not only because it feels good but because those with a higher happiness level are physically healthier. Unhappiness wears down the body, and unhappy people often do not trouble themselves to follow healthy life practices. Happy people are also easier for other people to be around and more resilient to change and difficulty. Therefore, while not all of our happiness is in our control, we should do what we can. From treating depression to acknowledging and dealing with negative influences in our lives to learning some of the skills of influencing our mood, the efforts we put forth to be happy are important.

Science is beginning to understand how happiness works, with imaging processes and other kinds of research, but Buddhists have been doing empirical research on happiness for thousands of years. It turns out that the two bodies of knowledge are very compatible.

The man we call the Buddha was given the name Siddhartha Gautama by his parents. Buddha means "enlightened one" and that is one of his nicknames, the one we know him by in the West. In the East, he is commonly called Sugata, the happy one. From the very beginning, Buddhism has taught that happiness is available to everyone, all the time, in this life. They don't just teach this in the abstract but have developed practices of meditation that help people develop the skills of happiness.

Buddhism teaches that happiness is only available right now, in the present, and that all we need for happiness is to learn the skill of staying in the present moment and returning to it when we are captured or hijacked into the past or the future.

It's easy to understand that losing ourselves in the past, whether in nostalgia or stress, is not a good idea, but sometimes people defend living in the future as planning and resist giving this up. We need our plans, after all! And if we are enjoying the present moment, which includes making a list for tomorrow, we are in the present. However, if we've been carried away into anxious worrying about what we'll do if this or that happens tomorrow, then we've lost the present moment and ourselves (and our happiness) with it. If we think about something that happened yesterday so that we can learn from it, we are in the present. If that memory captures us such that we feel those emotions and are carried along by them, then we've lost touch with the present.

If we don't know how to be happy in the present moment, we will not know how to be happy in a future moment. And if we can't enjoy our experience of the present moment, we will not be able to enjoy our memories either. As the Buddhists say, you can't enjoy tomorrow's glass of water because you don't have it yet. And if you can't enjoy today's glass of water, you won't enjoy tomorrow's either. This is not to say that we shouldn't plan prudently for the future or even make sacrifices for the future. It is to say that our happiness is now.

Scientific evidence also suggests that focusing on the present builds a better future. Everything we experience, including our moods, contributes to building preferred pathways in the brain. If we often get hijacked out of the present into stress and anger, and if we pay attention to those states and perhaps even enjoy them, the pathways built by our brains will favor anger and stress and make it more likely that our future will contain stress and anger. It really is literally, chemically true that we have to learn to be happy in the present moment to build our happiness in the future.

Staying in the present moment is one of the tasks of learning to meditate, but it is also a task of life that can be practiced anywhere. Buddhist teacher Thich Nhat Hanh, in his book *The Miracle of Mindfulness*, writes memorably about "washing the dishes to wash the dishes"—simply enjoying that chore rather than allowing our minds to obsess about the past or the future. However, a meditation practice is helpful because it gives us a way to practice the skills of staying in the present before we actually need them. Meditation is sometimes pleasant in itself, but it is mostly a learning experience. That's why it is often called meditation practice. It is a little like childbirth education classes in which expectant parents prepare for labor and delivery. It is possible to learn some of the techniques that make childbirth easier after you go into labor, but it's better to have learned and practiced them in advance.

Buddhists say that the task of meditation is simply to find happiness in the present moment and learn enough about what hijacks us and how to manage ourselves such that we have the skills to stay in the present moment in our daily lives. So you sit, settled into a peaceful breathing pattern, relaxed and alert, perhaps repeating a phrase like "breathing in peace, breathing out love" in your mind. You enjoy the present moment until—you usually don't have to wait very long—suddenly you realize that you've been hijacked. You are worrying about the future. You are thinking up a fine retort. You are re-living the experience of the near accident you had the day before and chewing out the careless driver in your mind. You're writing your to-do list. "Oops," you think, "I don't have to do any of that. Back to the present. Sitting. Breathing in peace. Breathing out love."

You do that for twenty minutes, bringing yourself back, over and over again, noticing where you've been, learning to recognize your own patterns, breathing in peace, breathing out love . . . oops, hijacked yet again! Starting over. . . .

If you practice meditation regularly, you will likely start to notice that you can do the same thing in your daily life. You've strengthened some new neural pathways. You know where to go when you need to stay in the present moment. Eventually, you will get so that you can go there even in extreme circumstances—such as when you have every reason to be anxious but just don't need to dwell there.

The world's experts on happiness, the Buddhists, say that the easiest way to become a happy person is to spend some time practicing happiness—practicing being simply present to what is in its most basic form.

Much of our unhappiness is self-made, through worrying about the future or dwelling in the unpleasant past or letting ourselves be hijacked by negative emotions regarding things happening elsewhere. Learning to notice and control this anxious negativity frees us to enjoy the present and work productively within it, to nurture relationships with the people around us and find meaning in the everyday work of our lives.

Activities and Questions

1. The essay states that happiness is only available in the present. Meditation is a way to practice staying in the present. For the next few weeks, meditate daily, saying to yourself "breathing in peace, breathing out love." Notice how your mind strays and gently bring yourself back to the breathing. When your mind hijacks you as you are trying to meditate, what do you do to come back to the present?

2. Do you resonate with the idea that your emotions can become hijacked in your daily life? What triggers that? What helps you return to yourself?

3. What is your relationship with your mood? Do you feel that your mood mostly fits circumstances, or do you struggle to feel

as good as you think you should feel? Is depression a part of your life? How do you manage that?

4. Sit in silence in a quiet place. Close your eyes. Remember a time when you felt pure, sweet happiness. Savor the moment. Remember all the details. Where were you? Were you alone or with someone? Were you much younger than you are today or was the happy experience a recent one? You might want to share this moment of happiness with your group.

5. One part of happiness is understanding what makes life meaningful for us. Ask yourself that question. You might wonder where that sense of meaning came from. Is it the same as or different from your parents' sense of meaning?

Thinking about the Words of the Day

Before coming to the gathering, think of a few words, phrases, or metaphors that describe your happiness. The prompt for the Words of the Day activity will be to complete this sentence: "Happiness for me is . . ."

~

GATHERING

Words of the Day

Happiness for me is . . .

Chalice Lighting

We light this chalice [candle, lamp, etc.] to shine on our time together. In its light we celebrate the relationships and understanding we are creating in this place and time. May our sharing be deep. [Light the chalice.]

The Basket

Responsive Reading

Leader: The words we share . . .

Response: *come from our hearts, our minds, our lives.*

Leader: The feelings we express . . .

Response: *are real, important, and a part of the human heritage we all share.*

Leader: The ties we create in this community . . .

Response: *remind us of the web of creation, of which we are a part.*

On Our Hearts   10 minutes

Silence   3 minutes

Shared Readings

If you're happy and you know it, clap your hands . . .
—Children's song, attributed to Alfred B. Smith

Happiness comes from qualities of being which cultivate an inner experience of peace, contentment, and fulfillment in the moment. . . . We begin to recognize that happiness can be as simple as the choice to stay in the moment and be at peace.
—Paul Epstein

It is the very pursuit of happiness that thwarts happiness.
—Viktor Frankl

Anyone practicing meditation will find inner happiness (harmony), the happiness that does not wither, the only stable happiness that will last indefinitely.
—Julien Bouchard

The turning-toward happiness as a valid goal and the conscious decision to seek happiness in a systematic manner can profoundly change the rest of our lives.
—The Dalai Lama XIV and Howard C. Cutler

Joy does not simply happen to us. We have to choose joy and keep choosing it every day.
—Henri Nouwen

Learning to live gratefully in the present moment will do wonders for our happiness. . . . Too often, people become caught up analyzing and replaying regrets of the distant past or entertaining worries about the future. As a result, they miss the beautiful symphony of life being played out right in front of their eyes in the present moment.
—Jason Thomas

Sharing   60 minutes

Closing Circle

Extinguishing the Chalice

We extinguish this flame, and we remember the warmth of our community, the light of our wisdom, the generosity of our sharing. We keep these in our heart until we meet again. [Extinguish the chalice.]

Song/Silence

Announcements

TWELVE

Spiritual Garage Sale

∼

BEFORE YOU GATHER

I have walked through many lives,
some of them my own,
and I am not who I was,
though some principle of being abides . . .
I am not done with my changes.
  —Stanley Kunitz

Religious traditions are far more like rivers than stones. Like the
Ganges or the Gallatin, they are flowing and changing. Sometimes
they dry up in arid land; sometimes they radically change course
and move out to water new territory.
  —Diana Eck

Oh, would that my mind could let fall its dead ideas, as the tree
does its withered leaves!
  —André Gide

Prayers and chants, images, temples, gods, sages, definitions, and
cosmologies are but ferries to a shore of experience beyond the
categories of thought, to be abandoned on arrival.
  —Joseph Campbell

The human being's attempt to understand the Creator is never static; it is constantly in motion.

—Madeleine L'Engle

Consider This

When a family or group holds a garage sale, they collect all the stuff they don't want any more, put irresistibly low price tags on it, and put it out to sell to people who, amazingly enough, will pay, if not good money, at least some money, for all that cast-off stuff. The sellers benefit from this exercise in several ways. They make room in their homes so that they can more easily move around and perhaps even have space to bring in something new. They also might find things that have been out of sight and mind and that now can be brought out and cherished anew. And sometimes, they can even make a human connection with those who are buying. But . . . where did all that stuff come from?

- Some things belong to another era of our lives, when we had different interests and needs. For instance, outgrown clothes, supplies for hobbies we no longer pursue, towels that match the bathroom in our last home, the bike we purchased before our knee went bad. These things are perfectly good; we wanted and used them once. It's just that *we* don't need them anymore. They don't work with our life as it is now. But for somebody else? A treasure!

- Then there are the things that we never used. Gifts that came with love but without thought, clothing that didn't fit and was never returned, all the things that looked great in the catalog or store but turned out badly for whatever reason. Lots of this stuff is still in the original box, never used. It never really belonged to us at all. Better luck to someone else!

- There are also a few things that once worked well for us and would still be perfectly good, possibly even usable, but they are broken and we lack the knowledge or tools or time or patience to fix them. The doll whose legs have come off was once beloved, and she still has beautiful clothes, but it's clear that only a doll maker can get those legs back on and, well, it's time to put her and her wardrobe in the garage sale.

When we think about a spiritual garage sale, we go through a similar process of preparation, except with our beliefs, ideas, loves, and fears. The furniture is not of our homes but of our minds and hearts. And just as it is good to go through our physical belongings from time to time, tossing what is outgrown or broken or just taking up space, so it is good to go through the closets of our minds and hearts to locate and discard the ideas and beliefs that don't fit anymore, have been broken, or never belonged to us at all. We can take those things to a sort of spiritual garage sale to get rid of them in good conscience. Besides freeing up some mental space, we might also find a few things that we cherish enough to keep in the forefront of our minds.

What goes to the spiritual garage sale?

- Things that belonged to another era of our life. Perhaps in our childhood we always needed to be on the lookout for adults who had been drinking too much and were going to be unpleasant and unpredictable. But now that we can choose which family and friends to spend time with and rarely need to scan the horizon for that particular danger, we can put it in the spiritual garage sale. We can let our approach to new people and new situations be a little less vigilant.

- Beliefs that never fit us at all but are still hanging around. You may have never accepted all the tenets of the faith of your parents and always argued in your heart with your teachers, but those beliefs might still be there, taking up room in the reject pile, still carrying a faint odor of your childhood worry and disappointment. Or perhaps what your best friend told you about sex, which you doubted from the beginning, still lingers in your mental garage. Or a powerful teacher told you what you could or couldn't aspire to, and that is still with you. You might have forgotten all about that stuff, but if it's still there it's great fodder for the spiritual garage sale.

- Things that have broken and can't or shouldn't be fixed. These could include the hubris of your young adulthood or the belief that only the handsome man gets the woman of his dreams or a faith in the goodness of humanity that, for the moment at least, seems broken beyond repair. Another sort of thing that gets broken is a habit or practice that once served us well. Perhaps there was a time in your life when you nurtured your spiritual life by journaling, but lately that practice has fallen away. You can't make yourself do it anymore. Time to take that practice to the garage sale and find something else. Or once you ran miles every weekend but your aging knees now need a gentler form of exercise. Fond as you were of that running, it's time for your attachment to that activity to go to the garage sale.

It might take a while to gather up a group of items for a sale like this. Think back to things you used to believe or used to think. What did you believe as a young adult, a middle-aged person, a teen, or a pre-teen? Do you remember times when you confronted an authority figure? Do you remember moments of frustration as things that seemed obvious to you were not shared? What were you told about yourself and your gifts and prospects in life? What were you told about gender and sexual expression? The proper role of government?

You can find candidates for your spiritual garage sale by noticing what makes you unreasonably angry or who you take an instant dislike to for no apparent reason. Those strong reactions often point to old mental baggage that we've not finished getting rid of. You can also find some of your most tender "used to thinks" by noticing what you avoid. Some people stay away from teenagers because they are so uncomfortable with the way they were at that age. The various crises we have weathered often have resulted in changes of mind or heart, which create a big discard pile of ideas, feelings, and beliefs.

A spiritual garage sale can also help us to connect to those around us. We can either share with them what we have found or we can relate to those who are dealing with similar issues.

The more imaginative we are, the more power our spiritual garage sale will have. If we take a few steps beyond identifying the mental items we plan to put in our garage sale and actually "hold" that garage sale in our mind's eye, the old stuff we intend to get rid of is more likely to stay away. We could do this as a guided meditation, picturing in our mind the collection of items, placing them on tables in our driveway, putting price tags on them, and picturing the people who snap them up as wonderful and helpful for their lives and drive off with them. The more detailed and vivid we can be in our imagination, the better. What color is that box of old political ideas? Does anything smell? Are these things neat? Cluttered? Do any of them make noise? Alternatively, perhaps an old idea that you've outgrown will, if polished up with a bit of nostalgia, work for someone else. Just because we are getting rid of something does not necessarily mean it was a bad thing. Most of our mental baggage is there because it served a purpose at some point in our lives. Identifying that purpose and summoning up some gratitude for it as we put it in the discard pile helps us let go completely.

We could go further by thinking of items that could serve as tokens or symbols for the ideas and feelings we are discarding. For instance, if we are putting in our garage sale the ideas about love that we picked up in romance novels and are now unusable, we could actually find a token with a Valentine heart on it to put in our collection. If we are discarding our dislike of dogs due to a frightening encounter years ago, we might find ourselves a stuffed dog at a secondhand store to symbolize this. All these items could be carefully boxed up and lovingly put in the trash, but they could also be put out on the curb with a sign, "Free to a good home."

The more concrete we make our garage sale, the more powerful it will be. When we engage in these sorts of symbolic, ritual, or meditative activities, it activates the part of our brain that does not know the difference between fact and fantasy. So while the rational part of your brain "knows" that this garage sale was all in your mind or was sort of a game with the neighborhood children who picked up your tokens at the curb, another part of your brain says, "Okay! That's gone!" Cleaning up our mental house is hard work, and every little bit helps.

In order to solidify our new decisions, habits, or ideas, it helps to have a concrete reminder of them. It is much easier to replace things in our minds than to simply take things away. So if you are getting rid of the idea that only a Barbie-like body is beautiful, consider finding yourself a token of a more expanded notion of beauty. Even the word *voluptuous*, carefully written on a nice card and posted on your mirror, will help you to fill the space that Barbie left. If your mental garage sale included the religion of your childhood, a token of the faith (or no faith) that has replaced it can be powerful.

Whenever we grow, change, learn, or come to a new way of thinking or feeling, we leave old ideas, beliefs, and ways of being behind us. When we are aware of this process and even let ourselves play with it a little, our growth is more solid, our changes come more easily, and we become more connected and compassionate people.

Activities and Questions

As you are thinking about what you might take to your spiritual garage sale, remember that that very thing might still be precious to someone else in the group. When you share, be respectful of others and of your earlier self.

1. Think back to an earlier time in your life, such as your twenties (or teens, if you are now in your twenties, or to your childhood years, if you are in your teens). What was your religion like then? What did you believe about God/a divine being, Jesus, suffering, death, and an afterlife? Have any of these changed? List a few of these to put in the garage sale.

2. Think about your dreams, goals, and relationships when you were young. Is there anything you are ready to put into the garage sale?

3. What has never worked for you that someone else might find useful?

4. What's a religious, spiritual, or cultural belief you are considering getting rid of but are not quite ready to let go of?

5. Think about an illusion or expectation about a relationship you're ready to give up, a mask you wear that you realize is not serving you well.

Thinking about the Words of the Day

Before coming to the gathering, think of a few words, phrases, or metaphors that describe beliefs from your past that you have moved beyond. The prompt for the Words of the Day activity will be to complete this sentence: "A religious or spiritual belief that no longer works for me is . . ."

~

GATHERING

Words of the Day

A religious or spiritual belief that no longer works for me is . . .

Chalice Lighting

We light this chalice [candle, lamp, etc.] to shine on our time together. In its light we celebrate the relationships and under-standing we are creating in this place and time. May our sharing be deep. [Light the chalice.]

The Basket

Responsive Reading

Leader: The words we share . . .

Response: *come from our hearts, our minds, our lives.*

Leader: The feelings we express . . .

Response: *are real, important, and a part of the human heritage we all share.*

Leader: The ties we create in this community . . .

Response: *remind us of the web of creation, of which we are a part.*

On Our Hearts   10 minutes

Silence   3 minutes

Shared Readings

In our journey through time, we all struggle constantly with what to bring along and what to leave behind.
   —Mark Nepo

The order that our mind imagines is like a net, or like a ladder, built to attain something. But afterward you must throw the ladder away, because you discover that, even if it was useful, it was meaningless.
   —Umberto Eco

There is plenty we have to give up in order to grow. For we cannot deeply love anything without becoming vulnerable to loss. And we cannot become separate people, responsible people, connected people, reflective people without some losing and leaving and letting go.
   —Judith Viorst

The Props assist the House
Until the House is built
And then the Props withdraw
And adequate, erect,
The House support itself
And cease to recollect
The Auger and the Carpenter.
Just such a retrospect
Hath the perfected Life —
A Past of Plank and Nail
And slowness — then the scaffolds drop
Affirming it a Soul.
   —Emily Dickinson

There is nothing like returning to a place that remains unchanged to find ways in which you yourself have altered.
   —Nelson Mandela

She may already have begun to see the things that would happen next, she was already the person she was to become.
    —Jorge Luis Borges

They have their exits and their entrances;
And one man in his time plays many parts.
    —William Shakespeare

Sharing   45 minutes

Discuss the Future of the Group   15 minutes

Closing Circle

Extinguishing the Chalice

We extinguish this flame, and we remember the warmth of our community, the light of our wisdom, the generosity of our sharing. We keep these in our heart until we meet again. [Extinguish the chalice.]

Song/Silence

Announcements

THIRTEEN

Leap of Faith

BEFORE YOU GATHER

Sometimes your only available transportation is a leap of faith.
—Margaret Shepherd

Whoever you may be: step into the evening. Step out of the room
where everything is known.
—Ranier Maria Rilke

To go in the dark with a light is to know the light
To know the dark, go dark. Go without sight,
and find that the dark, too, blooms and sings,
and is traveled by dark feet and dark wings.
—Wendell Berry

It is this belief in a power larger than myself and other than myself,
which allows me to venture into the unknown and even the
unknowable.
—Maya Angelou

Consider This

A man was climbing a mountain on a foggy day, and no doubt because of the poor visibility, he strayed off the path, slipped, and started sliding and rolling towards the edge of a cliff. As he fell over, with an enormous effort, he caught on to the branch of a bush that was growing on the edge and held on for dear life. He looked down between his dangling feet . . . and saw nothing but fog. The bottom of this cliff could be a few inches below his toes or a thousand feet away. He looked around. There was nothing to hold on to but the slender bush, which he could see would not hold long in the strain of his weight. Desperate, he called for help.

"Is anybody up there?" he cried, hoping for a passerby, but there was nobody. "*Is* anybody up there?" he cried again, his voice cracking under the strain. To his surprise, there was an answer this time. A booming voice from the sky.

"I AM HERE!"

"Oh, my God, God! I mean, God . . . oh, I'm so glad to hear from you! Help me!"

"I WILL HELP YOU."

Oh, thank God, I mean . . . I mean . . . what should I do?"

"LET GO OF THE BRANCH."

"What!? How deep is this chasm? I can't just let go! I might die!"

"LET GO OF THE BRANCH."

The man looked between his feet at the abyss below and around at the lack of other options and then up at the sky and yelled, "Is there anybody else up there?"

A leap of faith. The philosopher Soren Kierkegaard coined the term in the nineteenth century, and it caught on because, in the end, that's how it feels to everybody. I'm supposed to let go of what is solid and safe and obvious and leap to something else, something I can't quite see or completely understand? Right. Sure. Anybody else up there?

Well, actually, no. There's not. Not only that, but that solid, safe, and obvious bush is not going to hold you up forever. And yes, letting go is really hard. It's only a little bit easier if you are willing to notice and trust new voices from unexpected sources, but that little bit can make all the difference in the way you live and die. Has it ever happened to you? Of course it has.

Some people think that faith is something that only orthodox religious people have, and if they are not traditional believers, they think they must not be very good even at plain faith, not to mention leaps of faith. But orthodox and traditional kinds of faith are not the only kinds of faith and, as a matter of fact, every one of us has faith in some things and most of us find we take uncomfortable leaps from time to time in our lives. Every fall into love is a leap of faith. Every risk boldly shouldered, every social change imagined, every child intentionally conceived is a leap of faith. There's no living without leaping. Every morning when we get out of bed, we act on our faith that life is good and that our strength will be enough for the trials of the day. Every smile at a stranger is rooted in our faith in the goodness of persons. Every scientific experiment is based in our faith that this is a comprehensible world best understood by controlled, step-by-step labor at the frontiers of knowledge. Every garden we plant is an act of faith in the burgeoning life in the plants and in the competence of the nursery that sold them to us. Every night, when we let ourselves fall asleep we are profoundly trusting the universe, an act of faith that we utterly take for granted—at least until we are parents of toddlers worried about monsters or are ourselves subject to anxiety-based insomnia. And conscious dying is also a leap of faith into the unknown.

Most of us have fallen in love several times and changed careers more than once, and many of us have taken considerable risks to live out our social values because, by golly, that's just what we believe. Leaps of faith are not foreign to most us. We know that they are scary, but we also know them to be the price of a well-lived and rich life. Remember the song "The Rose":

It's the heart afraid of breaking that never learns to dance
It's the dream afraid of waking that never takes a chance
It's the one who won't be taken who cannot seem to give
It's the soul afraid of dying that never learns to live.

We understand the living death of such a constrained, safe, earth-bound life, anxious about breaking, afraid of dying, afraid of living, unwilling to give, unable to dance. Many of us are good at leaps of faith in every area except one, the area of faith itself. Then we suddenly get stubborn. When it comes to faith itself, we want to see exactly what is below our feet before we let go—even if we have no other real options, even if we hear a voice that many would call grace pointing in a direction. Articulating what we believe when there is no available proof can seem either unnecessary or risky, but it turns out that refusing spiritual risks is as deadening as refusing romantic, social, or personal ones. In the end, what we believe—whether in the goodness of God or Love, in the worth of individuals or the worth of living fully—helps us to shape our lives, take risks, and grow.

If we don't think of ourselves as "having faith," it is sometimes easier to understand faith as a verb, like hope and love—a human activity without which life is impossible. For we live our life by faithing, just as we do by hoping and loving. We hope for a future in which humanity has learned to live peacefully together. While that's a leap between what is and what might be, we don't talk about it that way, we just do it. We fall in love with partners, children, pets, enjoying the feeling and the meaning that these relationships add to our lives. We know that the more deeply we love, the harder the inevitable parting will be, but we lay that aside and love anyway. Taking a leap of faith sounds so risky. But living faith-filled lives is no more or less a leap than living loving or hopeful lives.

Just because we don't make a leap of faith into orthodoxy doesn't mean we don't have faith at all, only that we don't buy into the orthodox kinds. Virgin births and the God who sits in judgment over humanity may not appeal to us, and we can't force ourselves to believe in them, but we need to ask ourselves what we do have faith in and take the risk of leaning in, remembering and relying on the truths and strengths that faith points us to.

Do you remember, when you look out at the dreary landscape in the late winter, that there will be roses eventually? Of course, we all *know* that the seasons will turn, but do you remember it? Do you use it to give hope to the dreary days of winter? Does it bring you comfort? That's leaning into your faith. Spirituality—that elusive word and mood—means attending to faith, discovering and deepening and learning to live by what we believe. It's something we do when we realize that the bush isn't going to hold forever and that, one way or another, either anxious and frazzled or trusting and peaceful, we're going to slide into the fog and take our chances in the fall.

What leaps of faith do you take? Humanists take theirs based on the goodness of people and in the efficacy of the human mind. Any day's newspaper will test that faith, but they leap anyway. Many Christians take a leap of faith and imagination to believe in reincarnation.

It helps to understand that faith and reason are siblings, not rivals, two complementary parts of our thinking that create our whole understanding of our world. Although some disparage leaps of faith as foolish, irrational, and wishful, it is more useful to honor this intuitive and spiritual side of our lives along with the conscious, rational part of ourselves.

Ultimately, we must ask: What does faith offer us? The fellow hanging from the bush was going to either let go and fall to an unknown end or the bush was going to pull out of the ground, sending him to an unknown end. There's no hint in this particular story that the voice from beyond is going to perform a miracle for the hapless hiker. So what's the difference? In the end, it's not a matter of living or dying; that will be settled by geology, physics, and biology. It's a matter of whether we can listen to all the voices life offers and enjoy any ease at all in the falling. It's a matter of attitude.

The Zen Buddhists tell a similar story of a hapless hiker. In that version, the hiker is hanging by a bush and the bush's roots are pulling out. There's a chasm below and a tiger above, and the hiker, being a Buddhist, hears no divine voice. Instead, the hiker sees in front of his free hand a strawberry, a perfect, wild strawberry, and he picks it and eats it. It is juicy and sweet and tastes like sunshine. It is the best strawberry he has ever eaten.

Buddhists don't speak of faith or faithing; they speak only of the practice of living in the present. But the kind of trust in the way things are that is required to enjoy a strawberry while one's life is hanging by a thread seems to be a powerful, if non-supernatural, kind of faith.

So there was a woman who was climbing a mountain on a foggy day, and no doubt because of the poor visibility, she strayed off the path, slipped, and started sliding and rolling toward the edge of a cliff. As she fell, with an enormous effort, she caught on to the branch of a bush growing on the edge and held on for dear life. She looked down between her dangling feet and saw nothing but fog. She looked around and saw nothing to hold on to but the slender bush, which she could see would not hold long under the strain of her weight. Desperate, she called for help.

"Is anybody there?" she cried, hoping for a passerby, but there was nobody. "*Is* anybody there?" she cried again, her voice cracking under the strain. To her surprise, she heard an answer this time. In her pounding heart, a still, small voice spoke.

"It's okay."

"No! It's not okay! It's not okay at all."

"Just let go."

"I can't!"

"You can. You will. It will be okay."

The climber saw that the roots of the bush were straining. They would not hold much longer. There was really no point in continuing to struggle. And so she gathered all her courage and let go, and fell into the heart of the world.

Can you fall into the love at the heart of the world? Can you remember the seeds softening in the snow-covered ground even on your loneliest days? Can you smile at a stranger, work for justice, get out of bed in the morning? Then you have taken a leap of faith. And more power to you—for it is the only way to live.

Activities and Questions

1. Think about a time in your life when you made a decision that felt like a leap into a dark abyss. It might have been moving away from family and security, falling in love, leaving the church of your childhood, or something else.

2. The essay refers to having faith in the cycle of the seasons. Does that bring you comfort in the barren winter or parched heat of the summer?

3. Think about some of your religious beliefs. Which of these rely on a leap of faith?

4. What do you do daily that is a leap of faith, a falling into the love of the world?

5. Listen to a recording of Bette Midler singing "The Rose." It is available on YouTube and iTunes.

6. Watch a short film about a leap of faith in everyday life. Go to YouTube and search for "leap of faith short film, Dec 20, 2012."

Thinking about the Words of the Day

Before coming to the gathering, think of a few words, phrases, or metaphors that describe a leap of faith that you have taken. The prompt for the Words of the Day activity will be to complete this sentence: "I made a leap of faith when I . . ."

GATHERING

Words of the Day

I made a leap of faith when I . . .

Chalice Lighting

We light this chalice [candle, lamp, etc.] to shine on our time together. In its light we celebrate the relationships and understanding we are creating in this place and time. May our sharing be deep. [Light the chalice.]

The Basket

Responsive Reading

Leader: The words we share . . .

Response: *come from our hearts, our minds, our lives.*

Leader: The feelings we express . . .

Response: *are real, important, and a part of the human heritage we all share.*

Leader: The ties we create in this community . . .

Response: *remind us of the web of creation, of which we are a part.*

On Our Hearts 10 minutes

Silence 3 minutes

Shared Readings

To accomplish anything bold and beautiful in the firmament of time we must learn to change direction and fall gracefully.
—Sam Keen

A life spent at the edge of the pier is a life full of regret, a life full of fear.
—Ryan Lilly

"Lover's leap" and "leap of faith" are common expressions. Both love and faith require a "leap," ... a decision to take an action without knowing all of the facts or how it will turn out.
—Robert Beezat

When you walk to the edge of all the light you have
and take that first step into the darkness of the unknown,
you must believe that one of two things will happen:
There will be something solid for you to stand upon,
or, you will be taught how to fly.
—Patrick Overton

One of the great temptations of human existence is to base your life on contingency. That you will actually take the courageous step once all the conditions are absolutely and utterly right for you. When you have the right boss, when you have the right job, when the car payments have been made, when the kids are through college.... Of course, these conditions almost never come.
—David Whyte

The courage to be is rooted in the God who appears when God has disappeared in the anxiety of doubt.
—Paul Tillich

Sharing   45 minutes

Discuss the Future of the Group (if necessary)   15 minutes

Closing Circle

Extinguishing the Chalice

We extinguish this flame, and we remember the warmth of our community, the light of our wisdom, the generosity of our sharing. We keep these in our heart until we meet again. [Extinguish the chalice.]

Song/Silence

Announcements

FOURTEEN

Bucket Lists

∾

BEFORE YOU GATHER

Most people live their lives believing that circumstances dictate how they view the world. At some unconscious level they think, "The world has given me great cause to be fearful and worried." . . . If you choose to be worried, your mind will go hunting for reasons to be worried. . . . The same is true for gratitude: If you choose to be grateful, your eyes will open to the wonders of the world, and reasons to be grateful will come pouring into your heart. . . . *And you get to choose which lenses you will see the world through.*
—Lauren Rosenfeld and James McMahon

We are so obsessed with *doing* that we have no time and no imagination left for *being.*
—Thomas Merton

Suddenly, it seems everybody I know is in a big hurry to achieve their unrealized life goals before they die. Exotic vacations, skydiving, stuff like that. Me, I only ever had two ambitions: to be a jockey, and to play the title role in a roadshow production of Annie. Thing is, whether you drag your sorry frame to the Taj Mahal or throw it out of a perfectly good airplane, at the end of the ride, it's the same old you. I'm thinking the most transformative way to cross an item off your bucket list is to stop wanting it.

—Dave Maleckar

Consider This

Nobody knows where the phrase *kick the bucket* comes from. One theory that may seem likely is that when a criminal was about to be hanged, he stood on an upturned bucket, the noose was placed around his neck, and the bucket was kicked out from under him. Yet according to linguists, this is apparently not the most likely origin.

There's no controversy about where the term *Bucket List* came from. It was the title of a 2007 movie about two terminally ill men who set out to do all the things they wanted to do before they kicked the bucket. They raced cars and skydived and traveled to the ends of the earth. They also made up with loved ones and became deep friends. Suddenly, the phrase was on everyone's lips.

Most of the Bucket Lists you hear about are similar to the ones made by the two men in the movie: travel, adventures, indulgences. People want to go to exotic places like Thailand or Alaska, see amazing things like the Northern Lights or the Taj Mahal, do daring or exciting things like skydive or scuba dive.

Making a Bucket List is one important way to work out what you are going to do with your, "one, wild and precious life," as the poet Mary Oliver calls it. It is a useful and often liberating experience to have some goals and plans. For example, you realize that you really do want to see the play *Wicked*, which drives you to the website to see exactly where you'd have to go to see it, and you discover that it is coming to your town next year and you just have to make sure you get tickets, so you set yourself a reminder to do so. In this way, the making of a Bucket List serves as a clarifying exercise that makes it much more likely that you will actually do what you most want to do. Therefore, the best Bucket Lists are fairly specific. "I want to see *Wicked* the next time it comes to town" is different from "I want to see *Wicked* next year and will travel to do so." Putting a trip to Alaska on your Bucket List is only step one. Do you want to see the midnight sun or the Northern Lights? Polar bears or grizzly bears? Do you want to be pampered on a cruise or rough it on a mountain climb? Filling out details hones your list and turns your wishful thinking into a plan.

Yet, while it gives us something to look forward to, a Bucket List is a pretty limited form of life planning. The list of exciting things you want to do is probably not the most important list of things that will give your life meaning or make you feel happy or fulfilled. Trips, adventures, and indulgences can be the spice of life, but a different kind of list is required to make the whole meal to be satisfying. A meal without spices is a bit dull, but a meal of just spices is a recipe for starvation.

The activities and relationships of our lives that actually feed us are not the exciting one-time adventures of Bucket Lists. Instead, they tend to be the day-after-day stuff that we try and fail at and try again, all our lives: good relationships, satisfying work, the ability to have some control over our mind's ruminations and impulses. It is our habits of the heart and mind that make us happy and our lives fulfilling in the end, not really our Bucket List, as stimulating as the adventures it describes may be.

More than a Bucket List, we need a Being List—a list of the ways we want to be in our lives.

Minister and writer Robert Fulghum once reflected in his church's newsletter about another kind of list, his Christmas list. He claims to approach the season with lists of all the tasks to accomplish during the run-up to December 25. But one season he abandoned that approach and wrote a one-page Holiday To Be List, a list of feelings he wanted to have, ways he wanted to be, vibes he wanted to give off to those around him. That's a great way to approach any massively busy season, and a great way to approach life too.

What is on your To Be List? Here are some possibilities: a good parent to my teens, attentive to my mother, honest in my dealings with others, optimistic, faithful to my values, skilled in turning off negative thoughts, healthy, physically strong, an effective worker, wise.

The To Be List, just like the Bucket List, is most effective when it is fairly detailed. What does it mean, exactly, to be attentive? What will I actually do to develop the skill of turning off negative thoughts? What healthy habits do I want to develop? What does it mean to me to be wise?

Happiness is not found by going a lot of places or indulging yourself in exotic ways. The world's great religions all teach this and social scientists know it too. Americans, who, by world standards, have a lot of stuff, a lot of freedom, and a lot of opportunity to travel, are generally not happier than people whose lot is more limited. Happiness comes from the way we are, not the things we do.

And so while we want to focus primarily on our To Be Lists, when we do make that Bucket List, we can focus on the "being" component.

Why do you want to go to the Himalayas, really? Surely it's not just for the bragging rights. Is it, perhaps, to be awestruck by beauty and to experience grandeur? Why do you want that massage in a cabana on the edge of the ocean? Is it, perhaps, for the experience of feeling deeply relaxed and safe in the world? Why do you want to go to every national park, if not to be amazed?

When we become aware of why we want to do something we've put on our Bucket List, we give ourselves an important gift. We alert ourselves to what we most care about, and to ways of being that we can have in our own backyard. If we want to see every national park in order to be amazed, to appreciate beauty, and to experience awe, we realize that we don't have to go to *every* national park to experience this so deeply that it remains a part of our life. We don't even have to go to *one* national park. If we are in the right mood, there's enough at the local regional park to stun us into silence; there's enough in our back yard.

Because the term *Bucket List* is bound up with the movie about two dying men and the phrase *kick the bucket*, we tend to think of the things on that list as things to check off before we die. But actually, they are better thought of as field trips in the school of life, which we embark upon in order to learn or experience something that we will then find back in our own homes, jobs, and neighborhoods. We do the things on our Bucket List not so that we can die fulfilled, but so we can live better.

If we're aware of why we want to do these special things, then if we can't do them, we can find other ways to fulfill the same purposes. This perspective is especially valuable when things go contrary to plan.

If a trip to Paris is on your Bucket List because you want to practice your French and explore French culture, a delayed airplane full of people who speak French is not a disaster, just a diversion. If it's a trip to Alaska to experience the wildly natural phenomena of the Northern Lights, the fact that the lights don't show for a couple of nights is not only a disappointment, it's a lesson. It's not Disneyland, where the show starts promptly on the hour and lasts exactly forty minutes and is guaranteed with the price of the ticket. This is the world at its most real. It will happen, or it will not happen. It will be fabulous dancing curtains of pink and green light or it will be a gray glow. Or maybe it will snow. In the end, it is the qualities of personhood that we bring back from that experience: patience, appreciation, openness to reality, and acceptance. These are qualities that we will use every day at the grocery store. As Terry Pratchett says in his book *A Hat Full of Sky*, "Why do you go away? So that you can come back. So that you can see the place you came from with new eyes and extra colors."

We live our lives most fully when we think not only about our Bucket List but about our To Be List. We will most likely achieve our goals in both lists if they are not just lists but paragraphs that describe how we want to be and do these things, what we hope to experience, and how we want to see our world when we return home.

Activities and Questions

1. Create your Bucket List. Where do you want to go, what do you want to experience, how do you want to experience these adventures?

2. Create your To Be List. What qualities do you want to grow in (joy, love, open-mindedness, kindness to others and myself, gratitude, and staying present, for example). What would you like to be remembered for, what are you most passionate about?

3. In a TED Talk, Kathleen Taylor, mental health counselor, states that often people find their authentic selves in the final phase of life. She says, "What am I supposed to be *doing* with my life? . . . I think that's the wrong question. I actually think the better question is, Who am I *being* with my life?" Think about the following questions: Who is the authentic you? Who are you deep down?

4. What are some things you've had on your Bucket List that you've completed? What did you experience? What did you learn?

5. Have you removed something from your Bucket List? Why? How did that feel? (Consult the quotation by Dave Maleckar on pages 131–132 for a perspective on this.)

Thinking about the Words of the Day

Think about some items you want to include on your Bucket List, and how you want to be when experiencing them. The prompt for the Words of the Day activity will be to complete these three sentences:

"I want to do . . ."

"I want to experience . . ."

"I want to be . . ."

Prepare for Group Ending

If this will be the last gathering for your group, the second round of sharing will be a time for each participant to share about their participation in the group. Think about what you would like to share. This might be an especially important learning, a particularly meaningful gathering for you, or something similar. Also, for the ending ritual, you'll be asked to provide a word or two describing a quality you especially appreciate in each group member, so think about that in advance as well.

GATHERING

Words of the Day

My Bucket List includes:
I want to do . . .
I want to experience . . .
I want to be . . .

A quality that I especially appreciate in each group member is . . .

Chalice Lighting

We light this chalice [candle, lamp, etc.] to shine on our time together. In its light we celebrate the relationships and understanding we are creating in this place and time. May our sharing be deep. [Light the chalice.]

The Basket

Responsive Reading

Leader: The words we share . . .

Response: *come from our hearts, our minds, our lives.*

Leader: The feelings we express . . .

Response: *are real, important, and a part of the human heritage we all share.*

Leader: The ties we create in this community . . .

Response: *remind us of the web of creation, of which we are a part.*

On Our Hearts   10 minutes

Silence   3 minutes

Shared Readings

If you explore your true desires, you might discover that there are a few things you want more than others. If you keep on going in your search, you will discover one desire that has been with you your whole life.
—Noah Daniels

People make fun of me for my list. People just associate it with dying. They don't realize it's actually a way to live.
—Pat Palumbo

As our time on earth gets shorter, the list of promises we make to ourselves tends to get longer.
—Thomas Nelson

A legacy is what you leave behind for the world to remember. . . . Living a life with no regrets involves defining that legacy. You must create it yourself, for only you know what type of life you want to lead.
—Marion Elizabeth Witte

Remember, no two bucket lists are alike, but each list has the same end goal: to remind you that time is precious, and whatever you decide to do with your time should be thought out very carefully.
—Alex Wagman

Follow your bliss.
—Joseph Campbell

The bitterest tears shed over graves are for words left unsaid and deeds left undone.

—Harriet Beecher Stowe

Do, Be, Do, Be, Do
—lyrics from "Strangers in the Night"

Sharing   60 minutes

Ending Ritual

Extinguishing the Chalice

We extinguish this flame, and we remember the warmth of our community, the light of our wisdom, the generosity of our sharing. We cherish our memories, our learnings, and our relationships, now and until we meet again. [Extinguish the chalice.]

Song/Silence

Announcements

Leader's Guide

We hope that being a *Listening Hearts* group leader brings you joy and fulfillment. Your leadership is a special gift to those in your group. You will take care of logistics and maintain the process that ensures a safe place to share deeply. Your group will appreciate your leadership!

Listening Hearts groups focus on appreciative silent listening with no questions, advice, or judgment. This may be a new way of listening for most participants; as leader, you'll guide them as they learn the power of deep listening. At the first meeting, the group will discuss and, if necessary, modify a covenant that each person agrees to abide by during the life of the group.

Many groups feel a little uncomfortable with the lack of response after someone has shared. Assure the group that, in time, listening from the heart rather than from the mind can provide deep and meaningful benefits. Early in the life of a group, people often ask what they can do at the end of someone's sharing. The silence after speaking seems to be not enough. Some groups have listeners respond by placing their hands together as if in prayer and bowing their heads. In some groups, they say thank you quietly. In others, they nod and smile. These are all attempts to say, "Your sharing was deep, courageous, and touching. Thank you."

Later, as the group settles into the process, participants often remark on how the silence during and after sharing is a powerful, sacred time. The listeners have been allowed into the recesses of the speaker's life, creating a rich intimacy. Silence seems to be the best response. When the heart speaks and the heart listens, silence is fulfilling. The awkwardness is gone and the silence becomes deeper than language. This is a different kind of silence; some call it the fullness of silence. That's when people start to say, "Ah, that's the magic of covenant groups."

Your Participation in the Group

As leader, you are both a facilitator and a participant. You will go first during the sharing portions of the early gatherings to set the tone and show the way. Go as deeply into the topic as you are willing. Your courage will pave the way for participants to also risk sharing at a deeper level. Remind the group that wisdom comes from speaking our truth and being heard. Maintain safety in the group by watching out for cross-talk, advice, and "fixing." You should also serve as the timekeeper, making sure that everyone gets equal time to share. You can use a watch or a timer and signal the speaker with a small wave when their sharing time approaches the end.

Dealing with Challenging Participants

If someone forgets the "no cross-talk" agreement, you can refer to the covenant developed in the first gathering. A participant may consistently be unable to fit into the structured process of sharing without voicing comments or judgments. You may need to talk with this person after the gathering to make sure they are in agreement with the covenant. Sometimes people sign up for a group like this assuming that it is a discussion group. You may need to be firm in explaining that this is a sharing group, not a discussion group, and suggest that if they don't want to be part of a sharing group, they should probably not continue to attend.

Invigorating Your Group

After a group has been meeting for several years, it may experience a plateau. In addition, the "school-year" calendar may not work for all groups. In a recently conducted poll of small group ministry leaders across the nation, respondents identified four key areas in which listening groups can be invigorated:

Leaders. Finding, training, and retaining good leaders lies at the core of small group ministry. To do this well, try the following strategies: pair up new group leaders with veterans; recognize them for their good work—including through announcements on Sunday mornings and by a note from ministers (if the group is based in a congregation); and, finally, use various training methods to upgrade leaders' skills, such as role plays on dealing with difficult participants, a mini-workshop on emptying ourselves in order to be able to listen more deeply, or using a bell chime at intervals in the gathering to remind participants of deep/sacred listening.

Meeting structure. Tinker with the sharing process. This book recommends two rounds of sharing, with an opening ritual that includes a different method of sharing. However, some groups— especially smaller ones—may use one long round of sharing, while others might use three rounds (the third round being a freer sharing). You can also vary the ways the group observes silence together; invite participants to provide additional quotations to supplement those provided; and suggest alternative program lengths, such as mini-programs lasting three months.

Visibility in church. If your group is based in a congregation, everyone in the congregation should know about the small group ministry program by way of the pulpit, newsletter, and sermon topics that are coordinated with group topics.

Logistics. Ease administrative work by sharing the load, perhaps through forming a steering committee or inviting participants to assume leadership roles. The only core element that should not be changed is creating a safe place where participants can tell their stories to appreciative listeners who listen from the heart.

Deepening Your Group

As groups spend time together, they naturally grow in trust, which fosters deeper sharing. However, some group leaders want specific techniques for deepening their groups. In a recent survey, leaders reported that there are three components necessary for this kind of deepening:

Create a consistently safe space where trust can grow. Trust takes time. Leaders need to be patient to watch trust blossom; it can happen quickly for some people but take much longer for others.

Set a tone by sharing deeply. One leader told of sharing an unresolved situation in her life with her group. She was struggling with a decision to get hearing aids. She realized that she had to face her own judgments about growing older and memories of communicating with her father, who was severely hearing-impaired. She didn't share with the calm wisdom that comes with time and resolution of an issue but shared from the turmoil of the present. The participants sensed this and it increased their willingness to share from a deeper place—a real head-to-heart shift. Another leader in the survey reported that she always tells her groups, "I won't share all of my life issues with you, but I will go as deeply as I can each time we share."

Listening deeply takes time to learn. Covenant groups are a "ministry of listening," which can help us to listen from the heart. When we give the speaker our undivided attention, we take a step toward listening from the heart. When we notice that we are judging, analyzing, or evaluating, we have shifted from heart to head and made their sharing about us—our assessment, our thoughts. We are listening with our mind. This is the I-It relationship described by philosopher Martin Buber, treating people as objects to be used and analyzed. In contrast, Buber says, we form I-Thou relationships when we interact by being open to the other person with no agendas or judgments. We come into relation with the other, focusing wholly on them, which we call deep listening or sacred listening. Sometimes we get sidetracked when the speaker's story evokes a strong response. To stay in deep listening mode, we can make a note of our internal response to think about later, then return our full attention to the speaker. To be able to sit quietly when others are sharing is based on the premise that our quiet and patient presence plays a powerful role in healing. Deep listening is a process that we'll be working on for the rest of our lives.

Preparation for the Gatherings

Some gatherings have special instructions for the leader. These are located in the Leader's Notes for Particular Gatherings on page 153. Be sure to check there for information when preparing for the next gathering. The instructions for the first gathering are extensive and will require more preparation. Subsequent gatherings will follow the same format and require fewer instructions. Each gathering begins and ends with a ritual. Be sure to acquaint yourself with these. For the time of silence, you have several options for how to proceed. Try them all and add some of your own. Have your pre-gathering work done before people begin to arrive so you can be fully present to them when they get there.

For each gathering you will need:
    a chalice, lamp, candle, or LED candle
    matches, if necessary
    a basket about the size of a bread basket
    about 25 slips of paper, 1-inch long, cut from copy paper
    some pens or pencils
    a watch or timer
    meditation bowl (optional)

You will ask participants, prior to the gathering, to think of a few words or phrases related to the theme of the gathering. These phrases will be used in the opening ritual. For example, in the gathering titled Soul, you will ask participants to think of a few words or phrases that describe a soul, or their soul, and complete this sentence: "My soul is/is like. . . ."

FORMAT FOR THE GATHERINGS

Words of the Day

As participants arrive, hand them slips of paper and invite them to write a few phrases related to the theme of the gathering, responding to the prompt they received when reading the preparation material in advance. Collect the slips in a basket, then shuffle them so that privacy is maintained.

While this is taking place, recruit people for the tasks of the gathering. You will need one person to read the chalice lighting words and then light the chalice or candle, and another person to extinguish it at the end of the gathering.

Opening Ritual

The opening ritual consists of three segments. The parts that the participants need to read aloud are provided in the Gathering section of each chapter.

Chalice Lighting

Participant: We light this chalice [candle, lamp, etc.] to shine on our time together. In its light we celebrate the relationships and understanding we are creating in this place and time. May our sharing be deep. [Light the chalice.]

The Basket

Pass the basket around the group. Each person takes a slip of paper. Keep sending it around until all the slips are gone. Ask each person in turn to read one of their slips; you go first. There should be a breath's length of silence between each reading. Continue around the group until all the slips are read.

Responsive Reading

Close the opening ritual by inviting the participants to join you in this responsive reading

> Leader: The words we share . . .
>
> Response: *come from our hearts, our minds, our lives.*
>
> Leader: The feelings we express . . .
>
> Response: *are real, important, and a part of the human heritage we all share.*
>
> Leader: The ties we create in this community . . .
>
> Response: *remind us of the web of creation, of which we are a part.*

On Our Hearts

Invite participants to share anything that is pressing on their hearts at this time in just two or three sentences. Also acknowledge any absent members by saying their names and that you are thinking of them, even though they are not here. End this time by saying something like, "We will keep all these things in our hearts."

Silence

Each gathering includes three minutes of silence, which you should track with a timepiece. Some groups like to vary the way they experience the silence. Here are some options to choose from:

- Sit in stillness.
- Guide the group through this visualization: In your mind, go to a safe place, a place where you have known peace. This might be the woods, a sunny beach, a quiet spot in your church, or a flowering garden. Notice the sounds, smells, and temperature. Imagine yourself there quietly resting for a few minutes.

- Sit in stillness and silently say to yourself: Breathe in love, breathe out peace.
- Lead the group through the loving kindness meditation, or *metta*. This will take longer, approximately eight minutes. Say something like the following:

Today we're going to do a guided prayer or meditation that comes from the Buddhist tradition. It is called *metta*, or loving kindness meditation. I'll guide you through the four parts, each of which will focus our loving kindness on a different person. The first person you will focus on is yourself. For the second part, choose a loved one to focus on. For the third, choose someone you encounter often but hardly know—your child's teacher, perhaps, or a person who works down the hall from you. The fourth person you'll focus on is someone you are mad at or have issues with. I'll guide you through this, but before we start you need to have in mind your four people: yourself, a loved one, someone you don't know well, and someone you have issues with. Are you ready?

Settle yourself comfortably, and take a few deep breaths. The first subject of our meditation is ourselves, so open your heart to yourself. Picture yourself in your mind's eye as you listen to these words and repeat them to yourself:

[Speak slowly.]
May I be filled with loving kindness.
May I be well.
May I be peaceful and at ease.
May I be whole.
[Slowly repeat the above four sentences.]
[Leave a little silence.] Now, focus your attention on a loved one, picturing them in your mind's eye. [Allow a short time for this, then continue.]
May you be filled with loving kindness.
May you be well.
May you be peaceful and at ease.

May you be whole.

[Repeat and leave some silence before going on.]

Now change your focus to someone you encounter but don't know well. Think of their name, picture their face. [Give them a moment to do this, then say the words of the prayer through twice.]

Now, change your focus again, to the person with whom you have issues. Try to keep an open heart, and picture the person's face in your mind's eye. [Give them a moment to do this, then say the words of the prayer through twice more.]

Now, I invite you to focus on yourself once again. Say to yourself, May I be filled with loving kindness.

May I be well.

May I be peaceful and at ease.

May I be whole.

- Read one of these quotations to introduce the silence, then sit in stillness:

In quietness and in trust shall be your strength.
    —Isaiah 30:15

Be still, and know that I am God!
    —Psalm 46:10

Amid all the noise in our lives, we take this moment to sit in silence.
    —Tim Haley

In our ordinary sensing, perceiving, and thinking, everything around us exists as "outside" and "over there." We are spectators to ourselves and to the world. But in Silence everything displays its depth, and we find that we are part of the depth of everything around us.
    —Robert J. Sardello

I don't know exactly what a prayer is.
I do know how to pay attention.
  —Mary Oliver

Shared Readings

Go around the circle, with each person reading aloud one of the provided readings. Remind the group to allow a couple of breaths between each reading.

Sharing

There are two rounds of sharing. During each round, one person speaks at a time. The job of listeners is to listen deeply, keeping their hearts open. The speakers share from the heart as deeply as they are willing.

Round 1: Each person in the group takes five to six minutes to reflect aloud on the quotations, essay, and the subject, sharing their own personal experiences about the topic. As the leader, you should go first to model the sharing. Everyone who wants to speak gets one turn, in whatever order they choose. Anyone may pass. At the conclusion of a participant's comments, you may thank the person for sharing, but there is no further discussion, just a few breaths of silence. Then the next person speaks.

Round 2: This is an opportunity to share "second thoughts" as well as thoughts prompted by what others have shared. The speaker still focuses on their own thoughts, feelings, and experiences —this is not about debating issues. Everyone who wants to speak gets a turn, in whatever order they choose, until the time runs out. It's everybody's responsibility to ensure that all who want to speak get a chance and that no one is dominating.

Keep an eye on the time so that each person has an equal opportunity to share. Most participants will adhere to the equal time structure. Your group may develop a signal that lets the speaker know to wrap it up. Some groups use a timer to keep track, then signal when the speaker has 15–30 seconds left. The signal may be a small wave, use of a tiny bell, or a rain stick. Occasionally, as a group, you may decide to give one person extra time to share because of events in that person's life.

Closing Ritual

Participants stand, holding hands, around the chalice.

Closing Circle

Invite each person to say a few words about how they are feeling or an insight they are leaving with. When all have spoken, one participant extinguishes the chalice and reads the following words.

Extinguishing the Chalice

Participant: We extinguish this flame, and we remember the warmth of our community, the light of our wisdom, the generosity of our sharing. We keep these in our hearts until we meet again. [Extinguish the chalice.]

Song/Silence

You may want to end the closing ritual with a song. Judy Fjell's "Thank You for Your Loving Hands" is popular with many groups and can be found on page xiv. Your congregation may have another favorite song. Other groups prefer to end by ringing a meditation bowl or by sharing a moment of silence.

Announcements

At the end of each gathering, make any necessary announcements. Be sure to consult the Leader's Notes for Particular Gatherings, beginning on page 153, to see if there is anything you need to tell the participants in advance of the next gathering.

Leader's Notes for Particular Gatherings

This section provides leaders with additional instructions that are specific to particular gatherings. Unless indicated otherwise in this section, facilitators should lead the group through the order of events as described in "Format for the Gatherings," beginning on page 146.

ONE—SNAPSHOTS OF OUR LIVES

Before the Gathering

- Read the Leader's Guide section of this book found on page 141. Pay special attention to the opening and closing rituals and to the process of sharing.
- Bring a draft list of participants' names, phone numbers, and email addresses, as best you have it. Leave information you don't have blank.
- Bring name tags and a marker or two.
- Bring copies of the book for participants to purchase from you, if they need to.
- Bring small bills to provide change to people buying books from you.

At the Gathering

Update Contact List

As people trickle in, ask them to consult the draft list of participants' names, phone numbers, and email addresses and make any necessary corrections and additions.

Words of the Day

Invite members to write the words of the day on one or more slips of paper. This week, the words are a phrase that indicates why they were drawn to the group. Place the slips of paper in the basket. During this time you will recruit people for the tasks of the gathering (readings in the opening and final ritual). Ask members to check the roster for accuracy.

Opening Ritual

See pages 146–147.

Silence

See pages 147–150.

Business

Usually any business is handled at the beginning of the meeting and is quite brief. Today it is longer since you're just beginning.

Tell everyone how glad you are that they are in the group and how much you're looking forward to getting to know them. Also tell them the following:

- Each gathering will last an hour and a half to two hours and will be centered on a particular topic.
- You will meet for fourteen gatherings.

- Ask participants to let you know if they will need to miss a meeting or be significantly late. That way you won't wait for them or worry about them and can mention them during the "On Our Hearts" section.

Announce the location of the bathrooms and any other logistical information they may need.

Covenant and Ground Rules

Look at the covenant together, which is on page 2. Ask one participant to read the first item in the covenant. Are there any comments or problems? Can everyone agree to this? Continue through all the items in the covenant.

Introducing the Sharing

Explain that deep sharing and deep listening make up the core of a *Listening Hearts* group. It is a unique way of sharing and listening, so the group will spend a few minutes getting acquainted with this process. Ask three participants to read aloud one paragraph each from the Introducing the Sharing section on pages 2–3. See more information on deep sharing and deep listening on pages 141–145.

Sharing

Each person takes about five minutes to show their three pictures and introduce themselves to the group. You should go first to model. Pay special attention to keeping time at this gathering so that group members get into good habits. If someone goes much over six minutes, try to catch their eye or remark that they'll need to wrap up.

Closing Ritual

See page 151.

Leader's Notes for Gatherings

NINE—MENTAL WELLNESS

Before the Gathering

Obtain a recording of the song "Unwell" from the album *More Than You Think You Are* by the band Matchbox 20 to play for the group. It can be found on YouTube and iTunes. Bring the device and speakers you need to play the song.

At the Gathering

Sharing

Play the song "Unwell" at the beginning of the Sharing time. Then proceed with the sharing as usual.

TWELVE—SPIRITUAL GARAGE SALE

Before the Gathering

After the Sharing portion of the gathering, you will be leading a discussion about the future of the group and whether it will continue to meet after the fourteen gatherings outlined in this book are completed. If the group does want to continue meeting, you will discuss who will serve as leader. Think in advance about whether you want to continue in this role.

At the Gathering

Discuss the Future of the Group

The second round of sharing is shorter at this gathering by 15 minutes so you will have some time to ask your group whether they would like to continue meeting, and if so, how they would like to proceed, including who will lead.

You could guide this conversation in the following way. Remind your group that this is the third-to-last gathering. Say that it's likely that some folks will be ready to leave the group at the end of the fourteenth gathering and that's fine. But some might want to keep the group together in some way.

Some possibilities include:

- Continue your regular schedule, using resources from *Heart to Heart* or *Soul to Soul*, two other books by the same authors, available from the Unitarian Universalist Association Bookstore at www.uua.org/bookstore.
- Take a break and re-convene in the next season.
- Continue to gather but meet less frequently.
- Continue to gather but change the kind of group you have (some groups continue as informal social groups, for instance).

Ask your group to share about how they'd like to proceed. Make sure you invite comments from everyone. If a consensus emerges easily, go with it! If it doesn't, suggest that people think about it and agree to make a decision at the next meeting.

THIRTEEN—LEAP OF FAITH

At the Gathering

Discuss the Future of the Group

If your group still needs to discuss its future, shorten the second round of sharing to leave time to continue the conversation.

If the participants decide to stop meeting after the fourteenth gathering, ask if they would like to do something like have a potluck or share a dessert together to give the ending a special feel. If so, make appropriate plans such as setting a date and signing up for specific dishes for a potluck.

FOURTEEN—BUCKET LISTS

Before the Gathering

On a piece of newsprint, write the prompts for the Words of the Day activity this week, so participants can see them as they are writing.

"I want to do . . ."

"I want to experience . . ."

"I want to be . . ."

Note that the second round of sharing is different this week, so review it in advance.

In preparation for the ending ritual, write each participant's name (including yours!) on the top of its own sheet of paper. Then fold the bottom of each piece of paper up so that only the name shows.

At the Gathering

Words of the Day

As participants arrive, ask them to complete the three sentences about their Bucket List, which you have posted on a piece of newsprint. Then collect their responses in the basket and proceed as usual with the Words of the Day activity.

While participants are writing their Bucket List responses, spread pieces of paper out on a table, each with the name of one of the participants at the top and folded from the bottom so that only the names are showing. Ask participants to unfold each piece of paper and write a word or two anywhere on the page describing a quality or characteristic for that person that they appreciate, then refold it. Remind them to make sure they have written on all the papers! When they are done, gather the pieces of paper to use during the ending ritual.

Sharing

The first round of sharing proceeds as usual. If the group will not continue to gather after this week, the second round of sharing will be different. Explain that each person will have an opportunity to say something about what the group has meant to them, say what they have learned, or tell about a moment in the group that was special to them.

Ending Ritual

Randomly distribute the pieces of paper with participants' names on them. Let folks trade so that no one has the page with their own name on it. Ask everyone to stand. Then, one by one, have participants read the words on the page, prefacing the reading with, "These are the things we appreciate about [name] . . ." Go first to model.

Leader's Notes for Gatherings

Other volumes in the
Deep Connections Series
from Skinner House Books

Heart to Heart
Fourteen Gatherings for Reflection and Sharing

Soul to Soul
Fourteen Gatherings for Reflection and Sharing

Christine Robinson and Alicia Hawkins

In their popular Deep Connections series, Christine Robinson and Alicia Hawkins present a reimagined model of small group ministry. Their innovative program invites participants to explore a wide range of life topics in a format that promotes profound sharing and listening rather than back-and-forth discussion. The first two volumes in the series, *Heart to Heart* and *Soul to Soul*, both offer 14 pre-planned gatherings, each with an essay, readings, journaling prompts, and thought-provoking exercises to help participants prepare for the spiritual practice of sharing in community. With an easy-to-use format, each book also includes a complete Leader's Guide at the back.

Order from the UUA Bookstore
uua.org/bookstore or 1-800-215-9076